DATE DUE

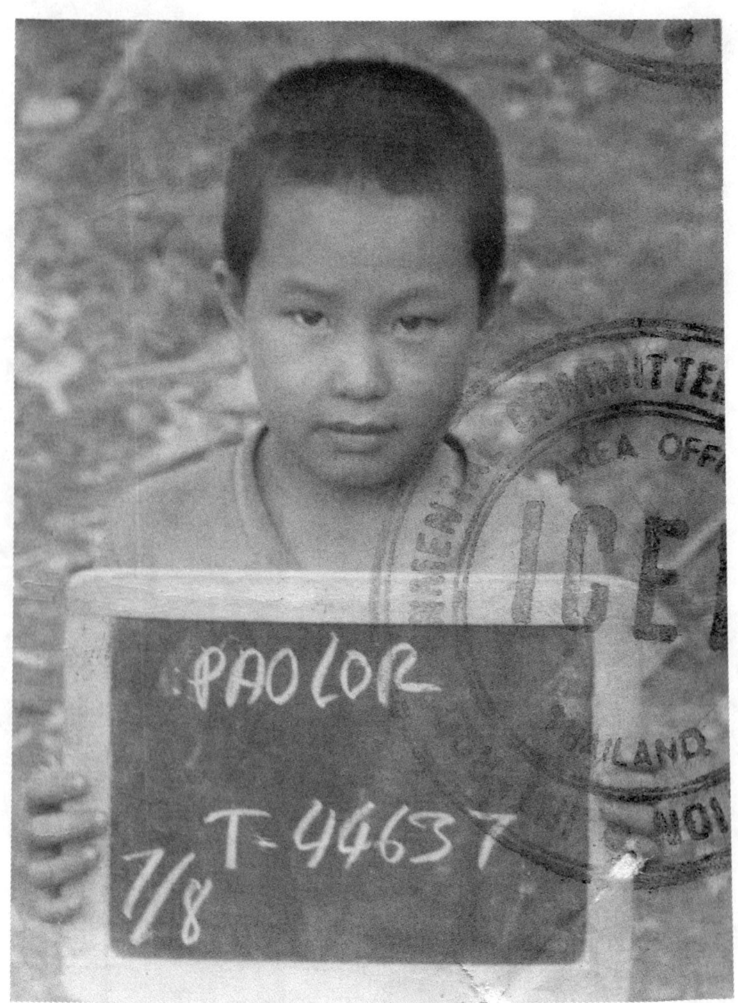
PAO LOR
T-44637
7/8

Modern Jungles

A Hmong Refugee's Childhood Story of Survival

Pao Lor

WISCONSIN HISTORICAL SOCIETY PRESS

Published by the Wisconsin Historical Society Press
Publishers since 1855

The Wisconsin Historical Society helps people connect to the past by collecting, preserving, and sharing stories. Founded in 1846, the Society is one of the nation's finest historical institutions.
Join the Wisconsin Historical Society: wisconsinhistory.org/membership

Publication of this book was made possible thanks to the generous support of the Wisconsin Historical Society Readers Circle. For more information and to join, visit support.wisconsinhistory.org/readerscircle.

Interior images are from Pao Lor's personal collection. The photo on page ii shows him at age seven at Ban Vinai Refugee Camp in Loei, Thailand, in 1979. The photo was taken as part of the official application process for refugee relocation. The map on page vi was created by Mapping Specialists, Ltd.

Printed in the United States of America
Cover design by Ryan Scheife, Mayfly Design
Typesetting by Wendy Holdman

25 24 23 22 21 1 2 3 4 5

Library of Congress Cataloging-in-Publication Data

Names: Lor, Pao, 1972– author.
Title: Modern jungles : a Hmong refugee's childhood story of survival / Pao Lor.
Description: [Madison] : Wisconsin Historical Society Press, [2021]
Identifiers: LCCN 2020054671 (print) | LCCN 2020054672 (e-book) | ISBN 9780870209598 (paperback) | ISBN 9780870209604 (e-book)
Subjects: LCSH: Lor, Pao, 1972– —Childhood and youth. | Hmong Americans—Wisconsin—Biography | Refugees—Thailand—Biography. | Refugees—Laos—Biography. | Immigrants—Wisconsin—Green Bay—Social conditions. | Wisconsin—Green Bay—Ethnic relations. | Wisconsin—Green Bay—Race relations. | Green Bay (Wisc.)—Biography. | Hmong (Asian people)—Laos—Biography.
Classification: LCC F590.H55 L67 2021 (print) | LCC F590.H55 (e-book) | DDC 305.8009775/61—dc23
LC record available at https://lccn.loc.gov/2020054671
LC e-book record available at https://lccn.loc.gov/2020054672

♾ The paper used in this publication meets the minimum requirements of the American National Standard for Information Sciences—Permanence of Paper for Printed Library Materials, ANSI Z39.48-1992.

Contents

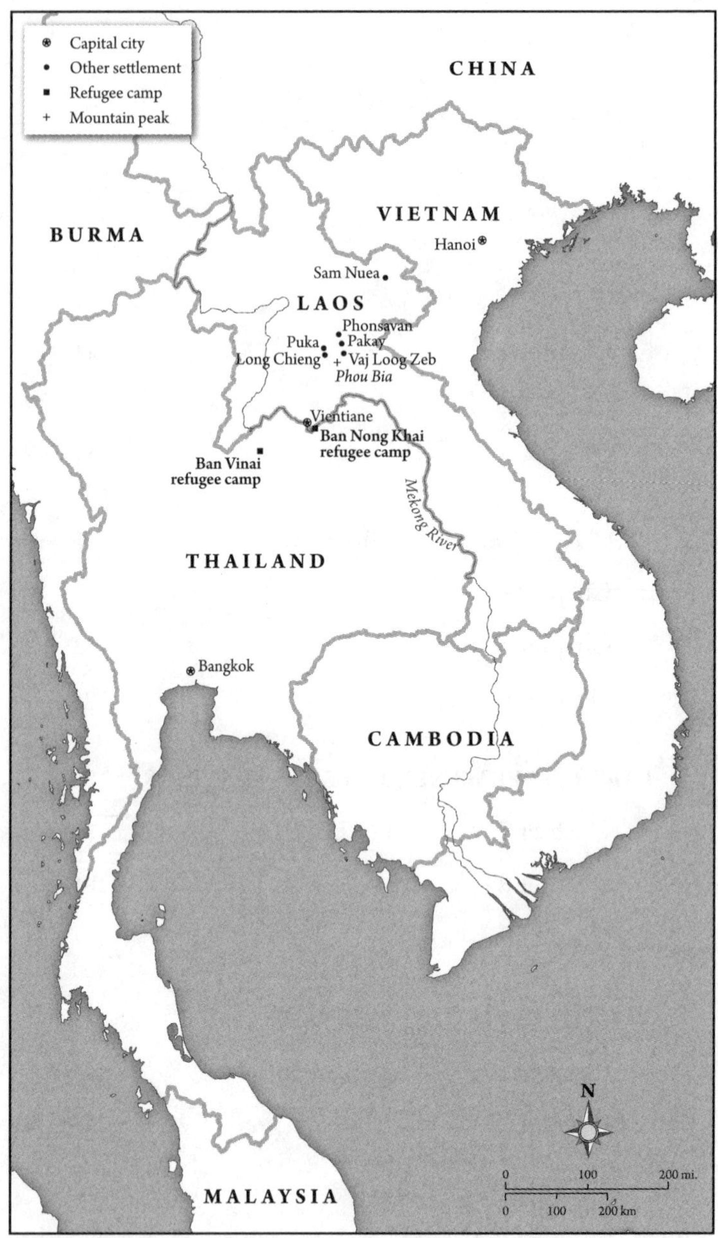

Pao Lor, his family members, and other Hmong refugees fled from their villages in the mountains of Laos through the jungle and across the Mekong River into Thailand, where they spent several years in Thai refugee camps before relocating to other countries. The locations of some smaller Hmong villages no longer in existence are approximate and based on the author's best recollection on this map of Southeast Asia, circa 1977.

Introduction

There is no easy walk to freedom anywhere, and many of us will have to pass through the valley of the shadow of death again and again before we reach the mountaintop of our desires.

—Nelson Mandela

Growing up in the jungles of Laos during the late 1970s, my childhood was one of isolation and tradition, then war and a long flight for refuge. Unlike my colleagues, friends, and neighbors who grew up in the United States, I didn't go to school, play sports, or celebrate birthdays as a young child. My days were taken up with doing chores, playing in my village, and following my clan and tribe through the seasonal routines of living and farming in the mountains. Not even the most forward-thinking person in our small world could have predicted what would happen to the Hmong in the 1970s or where my life would take me.

Almost five decades later, my family and I call Kimberly, Wisconsin, home. Kimberly is a small community about thirty miles southwest of Green Bay, a place none in the village of my youth had ever heard of. I live there with my wife, Maya, and our four children: our sons Sterling, Phenix, and Reeve and our daughter, Chynna. I am hopeful that Kimberly will be our home for many years, that my children will never be uprooted from their lives as their grandparents and I were, and that they know the kind of happiness that their ancestors fought hard for them to have.

Today, I hold the Patricia Wood Baer Professorship in Education at the University of Wisconsin–Green Bay, where I am also chair of the Professional Program in Education. Maya is a social worker in northeastern Wisconsin, working for Outagamie County Health and Human Services since 1997. Maya and I have achieved a level of security and success that twenty-five years ago would have seemed surreal to me, and even today I think of my life as an ongoing struggle.

A chance encounter prompted me to think about my past more deeply, to pause and look back on what I have been through during my journey from Laos to the United States. One day, after I had concluded a presentation sharing my life experiences and perspectives on the Hmong American diaspora, an audience member approached me and asked, "Have you ever considered writing a book about your life?" I was surprised and excited but also at a loss for words. I thought to myself, "What? A book about me? I haven't done anything worth writing about." For years afterward, I imagined what a book about my life would look like. I asked myself if audiences would find my life experiences intriguing and if there might be others like me. If so, would a book about my life help them? Finally, I wanted the book to serve a greater purpose, to be an homage to Hmong Americans, to refugees who may share similar experiences to mine, and to all the individuals, organizations, communities, and countries that offer hope and opportunity to oppressed and persecuted peoples around the world. With that, I set out to see where writing my story would take me.

I decided to focus the book on the first fourteen years of my life, when I was living in Laos, then in refugee camps in Thailand, briefly in Long Beach, California, and finally in Green Bay, Wisconsin. It was a time of loss, tragedy, and hopelessness but also of triumph

My parents are pictured in the 1960s in Phonsavan, Laos, in one of the few photographs our family has of them. My mom wears traditional Hmong clothes, while my dad's clothing is already westernized.

and celebration for me and my surviving siblings: my oldest brother Vang, my second-oldest brother Vue, my sister Yanghoua, my third-oldest brother Pheng, and my younger brother Kong.

The Hmong trace their origins to China, to powerful agrarian kingdoms established thousands of years ago near the Yellow and Yangtze Rivers. As China's imperial power grew, the Hmong came into conflict with Chinese authorities for control of resources, and eventually the Hmong were forced to leave China for fear they would be massacred. From China, the Hmong migrated across Southeast Asia during the nineteenth century to Thailand, Myanmar, Vietnam, and Laos.

For many years, my ancestors found a renewed sense of peace in the treacherous and unforgiving jungles of Laos. But the French, who began colonizing Laos in 1893, soon imposed harsh taxes on the Hmong, who paid in valuable opium, as opium poppy is easily grown on Hmong farmland. The Hmong eventually organized an effective resistance that won them greater governmental and local autonomy. Still, life was harsh. Farming,

My parents, siblings, and cousins in Phonsavan, Laos, in a photo taken before I was born. My mom holds my brother Pheng, and to her right are Yanghoua, a cousin, Vue, my dad, and Vang.

hunting, and fishing were difficult in the mountains, and groups usually moved from place to place every two to three years.

Prior to settling in villages near Phonsavan, the modern capital of Xiangkhouang Province located in northeastern Laos, in the 1960s and early 1970s my great-grandparents, grandparents, and parents lived in a village called Na Mai, which I haven't been able to locate on a map. Our contemporary family history begins there, and we often refer to ourselves as "the Lor clan from Na Mai" (the Hmong have eighteen clans in which membership is subject to birth and adoption). I was born in a village called Puka, which I've been told was near Long Chieng, an abandoned military city in Xaisomboun Province southwest of Phonsavan. The jungle has since reclaimed villages such as Na Mai and Puka.

In the mid-1900s, the Pathet Lao, a communist movement in Laos, and the Vietminh, the Vietnamese communist coalition organized by Ho Chi Minh in 1941, began to challenge France's hold on the region. In 1954, their combined forces drove the French out of Southeast Asia at the Battle of Dien Bien Phu. France's departure left a dangerous power vacuum in the region. In 1960, communism took hold in Laos when the Pathet Lao, backed by the Soviet Union, staged a coup and seized control of the Laotian government.

Afterward, in an effort to check the spread of communism in Southeast Asia, the US Central Intelligence Agency (CIA) established a military presence in Laos. The CIA supported the Royal Laotian Army under General Vang Pao, the highest-ranking Hmong officer in the army. In what is now known as the Secret War, the Hmong fought Laotian and Vietnamese forces along the border of Laos and Vietnam. The Hmong defended their homes and the critical CIA military base and airstrip at Long Chieng, rescued American pilots who had been shot down over North Vietnam, and conducted disruptive guerrilla warfare raids along the Ho Chi Minh Trail. During more than ten years of fighting, an estimated thirty thousand Hmong lost their lives.

When the United States finally withdrew its ground forces from Vietnam after the North Vietnamese takeover of Saigon in 1975, it left the Hmong to fend for themselves against the Pathet Lao and the Vietnamese. Immediately, the Pathet Lao launched a retaliatory campaign against Hmong leaders and soldiers who had sided with the CIA. A Hmong resistance group, the Chaofa, escaped into the jungle in the hopes of growing their numbers and mounting a counterattack, but they lacked food, water, and military resources.

Starting in 1975, thousands of Hmong fled south, seeking refuge in Thailand. For many, the journey required them to walk more than two hundred treacherous miles, over high mountains and through thick jungles while avoiding landmines, the enemy, and starvation. In 1977, when I was around five years old, my mother, siblings, two uncles, and their families set out for Thailand. Not all of us made it.

Life in the refugee camps in Thailand was challenging. The camps were overcrowded, with as many as forty-five thousand refugees living at the Ban Vinai Holding Center at one time. Relief came for many when the United States and other countries, including France, Australia, Canada, Argentina, and even Germany, began taking in the Hmong. Most Hmong elected to go to the United States or France because they were familiar with those two countries. Between 1975 and 2014, the Hmong relocated to America in waves, and some who initially immigrated to France later secured permission to go to the United States. My family left Thailand in March 1980, bound for Long Beach. Several months later, we left California for Green Bay, among the more than four hundred Hmong who immigrated to Wisconsin in 1980.

Over the last four decades, Hmong and non-Hmong scholars, filmmakers, activists, politicians, artists, musicians, and community leaders have captured and historicized the Hmong American diaspora. Many have done so to better inform the general public and the next generation of Hmong Americans about Hmong history. Their efforts have highlighted how Hmong Americans have made their mark on the American cultural landscape and embodied American ideals since their arrival.

What's missing are stories from ordinary Hmong Americans, those who were born in Laos during the Secret War and who relocated to America with their families. We need to hear from more authentic Hmong American voices who endured, survived, and triumphed against long odds during times of war and uncertainty.

My story is one of those.

Because I was born to an oral culture, it wasn't until I was older that I began to piece my history together, to put place names and numeric dates and times to the where and when of my past. It's taken me decades to do so, and some information remains lost, probably forever.

In this book, I want readers to experience the first fourteen years of my life as I did and as those like me did. I've been truthful to what I can remember, to what I saw and felt, though others might remember details differently. In the interest of protecting the privacy of those outside my immediate family, I have changed the names of the many friends, classmates, teammates, and other young people who came in and out of my life. Moreover, given that I was so young, I didn't always grasp what was happening to me, and perhaps that's for the best. I hope that Hmong Americans who read this will contribute to our narrative and to the evolving story of the Hmong in America.

PART I

Spook Heaven

One day, tigers will infest our land, drain our water, and gulp our mountains.

—Hmong elder

1

Our house in Kimberly is along the muddy shoreline of the Fox River, and I often stand in the backyard, close my eyes, and think about my parents, siblings, ancestors, and childhood home half a world away in the mountains of Laos.

When I'm near the river, I imagine that my mom, dad, and ancestors are with me and that they're my angels. Then I whisper, "I made it. And I'm okay." I used to weep in sorrow. In time, however, my tears became tears of joy. Even so, because I'm far from home, and because I've changed so much during my life, I often ask myself, "When I die, and one of my many souls makes it to the ancestors' world, will my parents and ancestors be proud of me? Will they recognize me? Or will they disavow me?"

I'm grateful that today I can stand by the Fox River, because it means that I survived my childhood. Many children I knew in Laos weren't so lucky, never making it to the "heavenly kingdom above the clouds where cities glittered of gold," which is what Hmong elders called America when I was young. They never lived in comfortable homes with electricity and indoor plumbing—or even learned about such things.

As a child, the scope of my world went only as far as the horizon and where my feet could take me. Survival was neither guaranteed nor easy and was largely at the mercy of Mother Nature. My childhood was a time before I knew how to hope or dream. It was also a time when, during the 1970s, American soldiers and CIA operatives referred to my little world in Xiangkhouang Province as "spook heaven."

The Laos I knew was ancient and isolated, beautiful, delicate, and vulnerable. According to the traditional order of things, there I was meant to become a wedding negotiator, tribal clan leader, head of a village, shaman, farmer, hunter, or fisherman. Where I was raised, daytime was for humans, while nighttime was for the spirits, both good and bad, who competed to influence people for better or worse. The transitions from daytime to nighttime, and vice versa, were thought to be imbued with the supernatural, liminal times between reality and spirituality. At dusk, the unseen and the seen, the known and the unknown, could cross paths, resulting in intended and unintended consequences.

In Laos, life moved according to ancient traditions and rituals marking such milestones as birth, marriage, childbirth, work, grandchildren, and death. To better our lives, to make sense of and bring balance to them, the Hmong established conventions, traditions, and ceremonies. We had soul callings, shamanistic ceremonies, healing rituals, wedding protocols, funeral rites, and other social practices. These practices brought us a fuller understanding of life's mysteries.

I saw the home in which I was raised as the center of the Hmong world. My house was shaped like a rectangle and was roughly the size of a typical two-and-a-half-car garage. The hut was built over large logs, one sunk into the ground at each of the four corners, one connecting the long edges, and another in the center. A gabled roof made of rice thatching covered walls of wooden planks or small logs tied together with bamboo strings. The hut had one or two entrances, a dirt floor, and no windows. Huts like my family's usually lasted about two years in a landscape where monsoons, oppressive humidity, scorching heat, and bone-chilling cold were common.

Our house had two living areas. One was where ordinary day-to-day activities took place. The other was for sleeping. We kept our scythes, axes, brooms, hoes, crossbows, and other miscellaneous items in the main living area, which also had a small space for cooking. Large rocks were used for cook stands, or, if we were fortunate, we had a metal cook stand. Charred pots were hung on the wall, and our metal bowls, plates, and spoons were arranged on a small wooden table. We ate most of our meals in the middle of the living area on a small, round bamboo table, seated on wooden benches only a few inches off the ground. Meals typically included rice and a main dish, usually assorted vegetables. These were placed in separate large bowls on the bamboo table, and after everyone had grabbed a metal plate and a metal spoon, we began to eat.

With the exception of my second-oldest brother, Vue, who slept in the living room, everyone slept in the sleeping area on bamboo mats. Above it was an attic, where we stored rice away from animals, especially rats, and kept other foodstuffs that needed to stay dry. In some clans, the attic was a sacred place where women were forbidden.

For spiritual and practical reasons, our home had no windows. Windows invited evil spirits, prowling thieves, or strangers into the house. I was most frightened of evil spirits, including terrible little creatures said to be about the size of an infant, with greasy black hair covering their faces. They hid everywhere waiting to scare people. They took souls as well, which they used to barter with the devil. Those who had their souls stolen became so sick that a shaman had to travel to the spirit world to find and trade for the lost soul before it reached the devil. If that happened, and the little soul-snatching creatures could strike a better bargain with the devil than the shaman could offer, then the soul and its body were doomed.

The most important spiritual item in our home was the round, smooth wooden beam in the middle of the hut. The beam was staked deep into the ground and connected to a crosswise log above the room to form a T. The beam was the center of our universe, the epicenter of our beliefs, and a gateway to heaven and the world of our ancestors. It carries weight with me even today, because when I die, one of my many souls will return to the beam and ascend to heaven from it.

Our home may have been small, but the world beyond it was vast and filled with huge trees, tall mountains, deep valleys, and an endless blue sky. I remember the sounds of nature and the feel of dirt on my feet. Near our home and village, fields of poppy and rice looked like scars cut into the land. During the day, I roamed around our house and the village, playing with toys, eating, napping, and sleeping. But many of my childhood memories are elusive. Between what I can and cannot remember is a haze, a mist like those that often drifted across the mountains and settled over my village.

In 1976, a year after the military had pulled out of Southeast Asia, I was living in Pakay, a village in Xiangkhouang Province. I was four years old and had been in Pakay since 1975. Before that, we had lived close to Long Chieng, and prior to that I don't remember. Pakay was like other developed tribal villages in Laos. Homes were built very close to each other. Rice and poppy fields were farmed nearby, livestock roamed about, and a dirt road divided the village in equal halves. An open dirt area served as a makeshift airport and a place for people to gather. We came to Pakay during a time of political and military unrest, so people were constantly coming and going from the village, leaving abandoned huts behind that other families could occupy immediately.

Shortly after we arrived in Pakay, the Pathet Lao, the communist regime then leading the Laotian government, began dropping thousands of leaflets from airplanes. The leaflets contained propaganda messages, urging everyone to put down their weapons and assuring people that the new government would help us recuperate from the Secret War. Then government agents showed up, establishing new social and political operations. They said they wanted to bring peace to Laos, explaining how their administration worked and how they intended to track the whereabouts of villagers. But it was clear that what they really wanted was to know which Hmong had collaborated with the Americans. The Hmong knew that if they admitted to fighting with the CIA, they would be found guilty of treason, which meant imprisonment, harsh labor at a reeducation camp in Laos or Vietnam, or execution.

Many Hmong knew they had to escape. Those who had worked directly with General Vang Pao had fled to Thailand with him in 1975, and around thirty-five hundred Hmong had relocated to the United States that same year. Most of them had reached Thailand without much hardship, paying someone to ferry them across the Mekong River in a canoe or boat. Thousands more were not so lucky. They had to trek through insect-infested jungles while avoiding the Pathet Lao and the Vietnamese. Some stepped on landmines and were killed or horribly injured. Others were captured, raped, tortured, starved to death, or shot. Infants, given opium to keep them from crying, died of overdoses.

My father, a peaceful man by nature, decided to stay put. He reasoned that he and his family were safe because we hadn't fought beside the Americans. In his mind, that meant we wouldn't be victimized. My father hoped that after enough time had passed, we would simply resume our old way of life. My uncles also decided to stay. They wanted to stick together, not wanting to repeat the mistake my great-great-grandfather had made when he left China and resettled in Laos without his siblings, suffering much for it. As for my aunts, all but one had already resettled in Thailand with their husbands.

After the Pathet Lao took over Pakay, they appointed my father as secretary to our provincial leader. He was one of the few literate people in Pakay, and it was an offer he couldn't refuse without risking retribution. As secretary, my father had to record the number of people in the village and monitor what they did and where they went. He also continued to run his livestock business.

~

Like many Hmong men, my father also harvested opium. I remember seeing two figures standing in a large field of waving poppies. One wore a red and blue striped shawl over a pair of faded black pants and a black shirt. The other wore black pants and a white shirt. I didn't immediately recognize my parents, but looking back it's clear I was watching them work. They walked through the field slicing poppies from top to bottom with a small scythe. From the cuts, a milky substance oozed out. Later, I noticed that the white ooze turned dark brown and black. When I saw my parents in the poppy field again, they were scraping the dark brown and black substance from the poppies and collecting it in baskets. That night, I watched them boil their harvest in a huge pot, then cut large black blocks into small packages, wrapping each in a clear plastic sheet. As I was getting ready for bed, I recall hearing my parents argue about opium in the other room.

In the morning, I saw my father outside. He was carefully placing the small packages into pouches that had been sewn into a large white cloth. Not far was a mule tied to a wooden fence. Once my father had filled the pouches with his packages, he placed the big cloth over the mule's back. Then he untied the mule and began walking it up a steep dirt path into the forest.

While my father was gone, I grabbed a dried poppy, cracked it open, and poured the dry seeds into my palm. Then I did the same thing again. When I had a handful of dried poppies, I popped them in my mouth, ground them in my teeth, and swallowed. They tasted plain, but with a distinct sharpness.

I woke up one night having to pee. Moonlight shone through cracks in the walls of our hut, lighting my way outside. Not wanting to go far for fear of evil spirits, I started to pee only a few steps from the door. As I did, I could see a small light in the valley below our village. The light appeared to be heading my way, inching through the darkness. I pulled up my pants and kept my eyes on the light, which eventually passed directly in front of me. But even with the moonlight, I couldn't see what it was. Eventually, the light worked its way up a hillside, where it vanished.

I was about to go inside when I turned to look for the light again. As I did, another light in the distance caught my eye. It looked like the whole side of a mountain was on fire, but it wasn't. Thousands of tiny lights flickered in the darkness, revealing the mysteries of the world into which I was born. I can't say for certain what I saw, but at the time soldiers and guerillas traveled the jungles at night, looking for or trying to get away from one another, perhaps using flashlights to guide their way.

I remember another day when I heard someone yelling "Help!" I dropped what I was doing and zigzagged around several huts toward the noise. I stopped when I saw two men standing at the edge of a pond filled with brown water. A dark object was floating in the middle of the pond.

"Go grab it!" one of the men ordered the other. The man jumped into the pond, struggling to reach the object. When he did, he pushed it toward the man on shore, who pulled the object out of the pond. It was a small child whose midsection was protruded, and I couldn't tell if it was a girl or a boy. The face was pale, the lips ashen.

One man told the other to get a shovel. When he came back, he began to dig into the hard ground. The men took turns digging until they had dug a large hole. Then they grabbed the body by the armpits and legs and gently lowered the child into the ground, resting the neck and head on a small dirt mound just above the hole. Slowly, the two men began covering the body with dirt. After awhile, they sat down on opposite sides of the hole. Suddenly, the child started coughing and water gushed from its mouth. The men quickly pulled the child from the ground, while the child let out a loud wail and started crying.

I turned away and ran home. To this day, I can't explain what happened, and I often wonder what became of the child and the two men who had saved his or her life.

A constant, rhythmic pounding noise stirred me out of bed one morning. I tracked it to a small hut, where people were standing around rectangular tables, pounding them with objects I didn't recognize. I couldn't see what was on the tables, so I reached a hand up and felt around. At the first table I didn't find anything. Then I went to another table, then another, but still no luck. At the fourth table, I finally felt something that shocked me. Instinctively, I pulled my hand back. One of my fingers had been cut and was bleeding. Undeterred, I foolishly reached my hand up again, determined to find out what was up there. Whatever it was felt cold and slippery, and it took me several tries to pull it toward me. Once I had it halfway off the table, I knew what I was touching—a Hmong butcher knife covered with lard. I did my best to get a good grip on the knife and pull it off the table, but it slipped out of my hand and fell between my legs. Before the knife hit the ground, it sliced my pants and cut a gash in my upper right thigh. The knife was so sharp that I didn't feel any pain. I was looking at the knife when someone started slapping my face, which was painful and startling. I ran out, figuring that I had experienced enough harm for the time being. I never learned what the adults had been cutting at the table, but I knew for certain that one had sliced into my finger by mistake.

The cut on my leg healed, but my finger became infected. More than once, I had to squeeze green pus out of the wound, which was really unpleasant but helped relieve the pain.

On another occasion, I found myself with several female elders. All were seated on small wooden benches around a dying fire. I joined them, but they didn't pay me any attention and kept talking to one another. Some were crying and sobbing.

For the next several days and nights, our hut hummed with activity. Many people streamed in and out. Others played strange music, striking a drum secured to a tripod and playing the *qeej,* a mouth instrument made of bamboo reeds. The music was very sorrowful, and I remember it touched me in ways that I didn't understand until I heard the sounds again when I was older.

When things calmed down, I learned that my grandmother had died and that the music and ceremonies were part of her funeral. My grandmother was among the last of her generation in our family, and her passing was mourned by many people.

The relative measure of peace that we had known in Pakay came to an end one night. I was asleep and then woke up being carried through the dark in someone's arms. There was no moonlight around us, and I couldn't tell where we were or where we were going. Then the person carrying me stopped, laid me on the ground, leaned me against a dirt wall, and vanished into the night.

I felt alone, realizing that someone had snatched me from my bed and brought me to a strange place. I curled up into a ball and tried to find some comfort in the dirt. Suddenly, I heard whispering. Then I felt someone moving around me. I was still trying to get my bearings when a barrage of terrible noises ripped through the air. Sounds of *boom, whoosh,* and *rat-ta-ta-ta* were everywhere, near and far, in the sky and over the ground.

I don't know how long the sounds continued around me. I remember a brief pause before the sounds returned, this time louder, closer, and charged with greater intensity. I couldn't do anything but curl up as tight as I could and wait for morning.

When I woke up, it was daylight, and I was in my bed. The sounds had gone. I felt peaceful, as I could sense that nobody was around. I later learned that I had been taken with my siblings to our underground bunker and that, within a few yards of our hut, fighting had taken place between the Chaofa and the Vietnamese for control of the region. The sounds I had heard that night were the sounds of war: of guns, grenades, and rocket launchers. I was thinking about this when my father came in and told me to hurry. I could tell he was serious, and I immediately got up to get ready. It wasn't in my nature to disappoint him or to be lazy.

Soon we were at the morning market. Our stall in the market was small, covered by a makeshift gabled roof of rice thatching that needed replacing every year. In our stall were rustic wooden tables and cutting boards, large Hmong butcher knives, pieces of pork and beef, and a few shoats. My father did all the preparation, slaughtering the animals and portioning the meat each day before his family was out of bed in the morning.

An hour passed, and the market began to bustle. People roamed the market shopping for their daily meals, medicines for all kinds of ailments, and other necessities. The sounds of butcher knives striking cutting boards, of pigs oinking, chickens clucking, roosters crowing, fish flapping, and people talking filled the air. These were all the things I could see and hear. What I couldn't see or hear was the fear, uncertainty, and hopelessness that had come to Pakay.

Looking out from our stall, two figures caught my eye. They were lined up to get meat from my father. Both wore faded green uniforms slightly covered in dirt, each with a gun strapped over his right shoulder. The guns were AK-47s made of metal and wood. Grenades dangled from their shirt pockets and ammunition belts were wrapped around their waists. As they got closer, I could hear their conversation.

"Those damned Chaofa, they definitely learned their lesson last night," one said.

"Yeah, they shouldn't return anymore," the other one replied.

After they got their meat, the men walked into the crowd. I

remember wondering to myself, "Who are these two people?" and "Who are the Chaofa?"

What the Chaofa, a guerilla group of Hmong soldiers fighting communist rule, were trying to accomplish at Pakay was not clear. At the time, I didn't know they opposed the Pathet Lao and the Vietnamese, and that they believed the Americans would return to support them in their fight against the new government.

A few days later, I again woke up in the dark away from my bed. This time, I was on my father's back. On and on we went before he finally bent down near a wooden fence, where he told me to wait. I waited there until dawn, when my father emerged from a nearby building holding a rifle. He grabbed me, then sat me on top of the fence. I watched as he opened a gate and walked toward several cows gathered a few yards away. When he got close to a cow, he stopped, aimed the rifle at the cow's head, and fired. The next day, my father and I went to a gathering. He brought meat and cooked other foods. My father could make anything taste great, including fish, dogs, cats, possums, porcupines, deer, guinea pigs, and more.

I started eating, taking a handful of sticky rice from a bamboo container and rolling it into a ball. Then I took a pinch of rice from the ball I had made, rolled out another ball, then dipped it in one of the dishes in front of me. I did the same thing until I had tried several dishes and my ball of sticky rice was gone. My favorite dish contained pieces of soft beef and a sauce with just the right amount of spices. I savored each bite because the meat mixed with the morsel of sticky rice was so soft that it melted in my mouth. It was the best meal I had ever had.

As it turned out, the celebration I attended with my father was held to mark the first anniversary of the new government's occupation of Pakay.

2

It was a cloudy, misty afternoon in 1977 when my father gathered my brother Pheng, my older sister Shoua, and me together. My father then told us to put on some nice clothes. We did, and though I had no idea why, I was very excited to be going on an adventure.

When we were ready, my father gave each of us a notebook and pencil, but he didn't tell us where we were going. Walking along a winding dirt road, we had to avoid many large puddles. Being young, I was tempted to jump into them, even with my nice clothes on, but I never did. Along the way, we passed a lot of huts, and I wondered to myself, "Who lives there?" and "What do they do?" To pass the time, Shoua and I whistled. Pheng tried to whistle too but couldn't. Only air went out from between his hardened lips. Shoua and I laughed hysterically as we watched Pheng, who looked more and more upset the longer he struggled.

We soon came to an open dirt area on a mountain ledge. From there, I could see a vast dirt plateau. Scattered over the plateau were several old, deteriorated, and razed rectangular buildings littered with debris. I could see inside many of the buildings, where wooden benches, broken chairs, and chalkboards were scattered.

"This is where you would have gone to school," my father said. I waited for him to say more, but he stayed quiet. Then he began to walk back toward our home.

When we got home, I was still unsure why my father had asked his children to bring a notebook and a pencil with us on our walk. He never said why, but I suspect he did it to remind us what our lives might have been like had war not changed them.

Shortly after my father showed me the ruins of what would have been my school, a terrifying night came when we had to leave Pakay for good. I remember climbing a narrow, steep dirt trail leading above the village. I was surrounded by tall grass and high brush, with many people walking ahead of and behind me. Parents carried their children in their arms and their household goods on their shoulders and backs. I felt confused trying to make sense of what was happening.

At one point, a barrage of powerful explosions ripped through the air around me. Shaken and frightened, I asked myself, "What's this?" and "What's going on?" Another explosion followed, then another, and another. Shockwaves rattled my body and filled my chest. The ground trembled from the force of the blasts, but we kept moving. Through it all, my father never seemed fazed.

Eventually, we put the explosions behind us. When we finally stopped, it was at the top of a mountain, where we sought shelter among many large boulders. My father put me down, and I remember feeling relieved to be on the ground. We waited among the boulders until the air quieted completely. Then my father picked me up again and we started moving. We walked until it was too dark to go any farther, this time seeking shelter in a huge, freezing cave. At dawn, we packed up our things and started on again, but this time I walked through what felt like a maze of forests, mountains, and valleys. The coolness and tranquility of the forest brought some relief as the leafy canopy kept the sun at bay. Still, I was exhausted and felt glad when it got dark, even if it meant spending another night in a freezing cave.

We traveled for days, walking during the day and sleeping in caves at night. When we passed or cut across a stream, we rested and gathered water. Otherwise, we kept pushing forward. Finally, we came to a mountain ledge. We could see a village on the plateau below, where many huts were packed tightly together. When we reached the village—the name of which I can't remember—my family found relatives, and we unpacked our things in their house.

While we stayed with them, my father built a house. A few days after we moved in, a snake got inside. My father grabbed an empty whiskey bottle, cornered the snake, picked it up, and put it in the bottle. He then went out, and I instinctively followed him. We went up a steep trail over several hillsides until my father finally turned into the forest. He found a flat area not far from the trail and started digging. Once he had a good-sized hole, he put the whiskey bottle in it. As he was throwing dirt over the hole, I heard him mumble something about not knowing whether the snake was a good spirit or a bad spirit, so he was burying it instead of killing it. When he had the hole covered, my father picked me up, and I rode on his shoulders until we were home. Only later did I realize that my father had shown me an ancient cultural practice.

Life in the new village resumed much as it had in the old. I hung around the house, roamed the neighborhood, and played with my siblings. Eventually, I forgot all about hiding in an underground bunker, the soldiers, the explosions, and the fear. Torrential rains and creeping mists were part of everyday life as they always had been, but they could not always obscure the sight and sounds of bomber planes in the distance.

I remember one morning when Pheng took me trapping for the first time. Pheng carried a knife and a few handmade baskets, along with other trapping equipment.

We walked up the same trail my father and I had used when he buried the snake. Before long, we entered the forest, struggling through the thick shrubs. Pheng cleared debris from several spots, then meticulously set the traps. When he had them in place, we went home. I was too excited to sleep that night. When the sun came up and it was time to check the traps, I dashed ahead of Pheng, eager to see what we had caught. Pheng moved behind me like a sloth. I quickly ran out of enthusiasm, and Pheng led the way after I slowed down. The first trap was empty. The second and third traps also were empty. I started to think we would walk away with nothing, but then I saw something in the last trap. I rushed ahead to find what looked like a small quail. Having never touched a wild animal before, I waited for Pheng, who lifted the trap and took out the animal. Then we turned for home.

When we got there, I showed my father what Pheng and I had trapped in the forest. He looked at it, then said, "That's not a quail. It's a chicken, and it probably belongs to one of the neighbors." I asked him, "Can we keep it?" When he agreed that we could, I was very excited.

We couldn't keep the little chicken at home, however. A few days after Pheng and I brought the chicken out of the forest, my father took it with him when he visited our in-laws—my mother's parents—in a neighboring village. Months later, my father came home one day and had the chicken with him, telling me, "Here's your rooster." I was in awe, not recognizing the chicken. It had grown so much larger and had new green, red, blue, and black feathers. Then my father told me, "It's almost New Year. Get it ready for the New Year cockfighting contest." Cockfighting is traditional in Hmong culture, and in Laos, cockfights were often held during the Hmong New Year celebration, which usually occurs in November and lasts for several weeks. In Laos, New Year was a time to celebrate a successful harvest, to ask good spirits for protection during the year to come, and to bury bad deeds in the past.

Pheng and I had never trained a rooster before, but we gave

it our best shot. We chased it around and tossed it into the air, thinking that would be enough to build up the rooster's fighting spirit. When we decided our rooster had enough training, we arranged a cockfight with another rooster from across the valley. I was shocked when I saw the other rooster. It was much smaller than ours and had mostly black and red feathers.

Before the fight started, a small crowd gathered at the center of an open dirt area surrounded by several huts. Not knowing what we were doing, we imitated what the other owner did with his rooster. We flapped its wings; tossed it around; pushed it toward the ground; massaged its back, wings, and thighs; and wetted its head and body. After the roosters were warmed up, they were simultaneously released into the center of the ring. Instinctively, they attacked each other, flapping their wings, jumping and kicking, jabbing with their claws, and pecking with their beaks.

Suddenly, our rooster retreated. It scurried toward some onlookers and began weaving through the crowd. The other owner grabbed his rooster to prevent it from chasing after ours, which ran into some nearby bushes. Pheng had to dive in after it, coming out with the rooster in his arms, caressing it to calm it down.

We walked home disappointed that the smaller rooster had put up the bigger fight.

I have a similar childhood memory involving animals much larger than chickens. One day, my father and I visited one of his friends in a nearby village. Sitting quietly on a bamboo bed by the door, I fell asleep. I was alone when I woke up, feeling scared and nervously waiting for my father to return. When he showed up, my father took me to a huge dirt field at the edge of the village near the tree line. Small groups of three to five people were scattered around the field, while individuals and other groups gathered at the wooden fence separating the field from a dirt road.

We found a spot near the fence, where I could see the whole field. Suddenly, two people emerged out of the crowd, each leading a huge bull. Like cockfighting, bullfighting is traditional in the Hmong world. The bulls were led toward the center of the dirt field. Slowly, their handlers got the bulls ready to fight. Inch by inch, they brought the bulls closer together until their noses nearly touched. Then the handlers released their bulls, and the fight was on. For a few seconds, the bulls sized each other up. Then they tore into each other with their horns and hammered at each other with their heads. When one bull backed up and charged into his opponent, the other did the same.

Finally, just as both bulls were about to charge, one suddenly turned and rumbled toward the forest. Immediately, the owner of the winning bull grabbed his animal by the nose ring to prevent him from giving chase.

When New Year arrived, I dreaded that my rooster would lose again. At the competition, I was surprised, and felt a little better about my rooster's chances, when I learned there were only eight birds competing and that mine was the biggest. This time, my rooster won its first fight. Then its second. And, in the final round, he won again and was the champion!

The next morning, I stood near our doorstep to watch the New Year celebration on the lower plateau. I was fascinated by the traditional Hmong clothes and the bands of dangling French coins wrapped around people's waists and shoulders. Even from afar, I could hear the tinny and clinking sounds the shiny coins made when rattling around. New Year celebrations went on like that for several more days. When they finally wound down, people slowly returned to their lives—to the harvest, the hard work of sustaining life in the mountains, and their daily chores. We were no different.

A few days after New Year, I stood on the edge of the plateau and watched four people carry a stretcher on their shoulders. Curious, I ran down to get a closer look.

Many people had arrived by the time I got there, gathering around the stretcher. Most of them were talking, but I couldn't make out what they were saying. People were crying and sobbing. There was a person on the stretcher. The body wore a black shirt, black pants, and red, blue, and green sashes around its waist draped to the knees. The face was dark, almost black, and rotting, a dark liquid oozing all over it. A huge swollen tongue stuck into the air.

I turned away, went through the crowd, and scrambled home. I had witnessed a funeral procession. The people carrying the stretcher and the crowd around them were going to the burial site. Along the way, they made a ritualistic stop, which has a story behind it. Long ago, there was an aunt who was late to her nephew's funeral. As luck would have it, on her way there, she ran into the funeral party. She asked if she could have some time with her nephew. She wanted to kill a cow so that her nephew would have it in the afterlife, and the family agreed. Since that day, the stop has become a funeral ritual in some Hmong clans, a last opportunity for relatives who might not have made it to the funeral to say their goodbyes.

Sometime after my encounter with the dead person, I came across a different but no less startling kind of death. One morning, I found my mom sitting on a wooden chair in the corner of the house, cleaning my champion rooster! Then I found out why: we were going to move again, and we needed the rooster for food. The elders claimed that we were no longer safe in our village, for the same reason that we had to leave Pakay. The Laotian government and their Vietnamese allies had attacked Pakay and were now rounding up Hmong men and taking them to a reeducation camp in Sam Nuea, or "Northern Swamp," a tribal village in Houaphanh Province near the border of Laos and Vietnam. We had to escape as quickly as possible.

After many days and nights of travel, we reached our new village in Xiangkhouang Province, called Vaj Loog Zeb, or "Rock Garden." It was located near the base of Phou Bia, the highest mountain in Laos. The location was chosen for its strategic and defensive position, as it could be accessed only from the west and east by single entrances. The rugged and secluded terrain made for a seemingly perfect stronghold.

My family took up one of the abandoned huts. Before we moved in, my father blessed our new house, staking our claim to the hut and warding off any evil spirits inside. He also asked good spirits and our ancestors to protect us.

It didn't take me long to realize that life in Vaj Loog Zeb would be harsh. Given the landscape, it was difficult to raise crops, and we were always low on food. Life was more uncertain, and I began to feel a sense of hopelessness and isolation. Dried fruits my mother prepared, especially sliced bananas, brought some comfort.

To pass the time and make ourselves useful, Pheng and I tried trapping again. When we weren't trapping, we played with other kids in the village. Our favorite game was "war in the jungle." We each held a fake gun that we had made out of bamboo. For ammunition, we used berries. To fire the gun, you put a berry inside a bamboo tube, aimed, then shoved a rod through the tube. Obviously, the easiest way to hit an enemy was to get as close as possible to him. Being one of the youngest kids, I got hit a lot.

When we tired of playing war in the jungle, we chased and captured little yellow birds about the size of a large coin. We would spread out, then move among the bushes, shrubs, and trees. Inevitably, someone would shout, "Over here!" and all the kids would come running. "Where is it?" we all asked. "There!"

a kid would say, pointing into the bushes. Then someone would poke a stick into the bushes until the bird flew out, made for another bush, and the process repeated itself. At some point, the exhausted bird would usually fly into an open dirt field, where it would land. When that happened, one of the kids would approach the bird carefully, pick it up, and take it for cooking. We never captured enough birds in this way for a decent meal, but it was better than nothing.

3

My father often went on long business trips for salt and other goods. Whenever he returned, I was excited to see him because he usually brought us treats. My favorite was brown sugar cubes, which I liked to eat with a bowl of rice and water. I always tried to make mine last as long as possible, stashing whatever I could away from my siblings.

One night, after distributing goods to our neighbors, my father returned home late. Though it was already dark, I remember Vue was still up sitting on our small bamboo bed near the south entrance to our hut, cleaning his gun by flashlight, while my mother was sleeping close to my other siblings in the bedroom. Pheng and I were still awake, waiting for our father so that we could gather by the firepit and chat before going to bed. Once he arrived, we sat on a long, wood bench with a crackling fire in front of us, with my father between Pheng and me.

At some point, I blacked out. When I regained consciousness, now in darkness, I realized I was no longer by the fire. I was lying on the ground, the rough surface digging into my back. Rolling onto my side, I noticed someone next to me. I felt his warmth and heard him gasping for air. But in the darkness, I couldn't tell what was happening. Soon the gasping ceased, and the warmth was gone. Later I realized it was my father, who had carried us to the storage room to hide.

I remember hearing gunshots just outside our hut while lying there. Blood rushed through me, and my body felt like it was burning. Later I saw streaks of light shining through the vertical cracks in our walls, as someone fired flares to provide temporary light. Outside the house, I could hear people whispering, yelling, and running. When I concentrated, I was able to make out some of what they were saying. Amid the noise, I recognized my mother's voice, crying hysterically and wailing, "Somebody has assassinated Vayeng!"

Her husband, my father, was dead, though I was still too young to understand what that meant or why he had been killed. Decades later, I heard a rumor that the Chaofa had sent the assassin because Chaofa leaders were convinced that my father had sided with the communists. Because my father had been a secretary, the Chaofa worried that he was providing the Pathet Lao and the Vietnamese valuable information about the resistance.

The next morning, people moved in and out of our hut. I had no real understanding of what all the commotion was about, so I just milled around the crowds or stood out of the way.

Then a group of men gathered near the center of the hut, and I followed them when they left. On the north side of the house, they stopped, and then two men moved to inspect a mound situated across from our cooking fire, where my father, Pheng, and I had been sitting the night before. One of the men started digging through the mound, looking for the bullet that had killed my father, while another said, "If the bullet had hit a little lower on his chest, Vayeng would have survived." The digging man kept going, deeper and deeper, until at last he stopped, unable to find what he was looking for.

Later in the day, I saw my father, but now he was lying on a wooden stretcher on the floor near the firepit, wearing unfamiliar clothing. The clothes looked very similar to those worn by the corpse I had seen months earlier. "Why isn't he up and busy doing his usual stuff?" I wondered. The next time I saw my father's body, it was still on the wooden stretcher, but now the stretcher was hung at about the height of my head against the north wall of our home. Still unable to comprehend what had happened, I kept busy playing with friends and cousins.

My mother stayed beside my father during those days, rarely leaving his side. She softly stroked his hair, moving her hand over the top of his head. Other women also came and went, watching and guarding my father, some swatting away the flies. One time, I heard my mother tell my father, "Please hold on." During this time as well, the mournful tones of the *qeej* and the funeral drum filled the air.

One morning, a woman I had never seen before and whose identity I never learned, appeared at the door. She immediately ran toward my father, wailing an eerie lament. She stood over my father, wiping tears from her eyes. And, like many others, she brushed my father's hair and face with her hand. Others in the house spoke softly, "He held on. He didn't deteriorate." At the time, I didn't know what they meant, but I learned later that they were referring to how my father's body hadn't decomposed as rapidly as it should have, which mourners interpreted to mean that my father was trying to comfort my mother after his death.

Shortly thereafter, someone grabbed me and told me I needed to go outside. Soon a group of men emerged from the hut, each shouldering a corner of the wooden stretcher my father was on. Many people started to cry. As the four men passed me, an overwhelming feeling of emptiness struck me, and tears ran down my cheeks. Sorrow had introduced itself to me, though I didn't fully understand why.

We followed my father's body into the jungle. When we reached several large mounds covered with rocks, moss, and shrubs, we stopped over a hole that had already been dug. Inside the hole was a wooden casket. The four men carefully placed my father onto the ground near the hole, and an old man proceeded to perform the funerary rites. Afterward, my father was laid in the casket, then the old man began slashing at my father's clothes with a knife. When he finished, several men covered the casket and nailed it shut. Finally, the old man with the knife slashed the casket several times. With that, people began taking turns covering the hole with dirt. They then stacked many small rocks in a mound on top of the grave. The funerary rites were to wish my father well on his journey to the spiritual and ancestral worlds and his reincarnation. The mound of rocks was placed on the grave so it would resemble a Chinese grave, just as the old man had slashed my father's clothes, shoes, and coffin so that grave robbers would think my father was Chinese and leave his body alone.

Then we left, heading home to a place of good memories and heartfelt tragedy.

Though he had only about a third-grade education, my father was the member of our family who knew the most about reading and writing in Lao and French. When he was in his early teens, French missionaries built a school in Laos near his village close to the Vietnamese border. That's not to say it was easy for my father to get to school. It took him nearly an entire morning to navigate the forests, streams, mountains, and valleys between his village and the French school. Still, my grandfather, an opium grower and addict, saw the school as a place where his children might have better fortunes than his own. Villagers openly ridiculed my grandfather for being an addict, and he wished to spare his children a similar fate. On mornings when my father went to school, my grandfather prepared a lunch for him that included one of his favorite treats—brown sugar cubes. My father was expected to be home before the end of the day or risk missing dinner if he was late.

Of course, the French had their reasons for building the school near my father's village. In their attempts to colonize Southeast Asia, the French tried to make some Asian cultures more French.

My father's schooling, however, was short lived, ending when the French were driven out of Indochina after they were defeated by the Vietminh and Pathet Lao at the Battle of Dien Bien Phu in 1954. As the missionaries were leaving Laos, one asked my father if he would be willing to go to France. My father refused, though I never learned why.

After my father was killed, many villagers left Vaj Loog Zeb. It was as though his assassination had cursed the place. With the others, my family also packed up and relocated, on the move yet again. Traveling through the mountains one day, an elder told us that, to seek safe passage and to propitiate mountain spirits, each of us had to pick up a stick and toss it on an already huge pile of sticks nearby. The pile looked as if it had been there for years, and many of the sticks at the bottom were rotten. We threw our sticks on the pile, asking the spirits of the mountain for protection on our journey. My mom told us a brief story about the sticks. She said that the sticks symbolized penises, and that a long time ago a princess fell ill and died on that mountain. The princess died heartbroken because her parents prevented her from marrying and ever sleeping with the man she loved.

One day, on a bright afternoon, after many days and nights of miserable travel, some people began gathering at the edge of a cliff. I walked over to them, and from the edge I could see a village with many huts. Suddenly, a group of strangers emerged out of the forest. They approached us and greeted our elders with pleasantries, and then we followed them to their village below. There were no empty huts, so we had to build our own, staying with relatives in the meantime.

It was our first shelter without my father. My mother and older siblings put it together. It was no bigger than a two-car garage, roughly patched together with branches and covered with rice thatches. Already, I had forgotten my father's presence, more concerned that we were again living on our own. Life was hard, made more so because, being new to the village, we couldn't immediately claim ownership to any nearby farmland or rice paddies. Fortunately, we eventually found some land to farm.

The village was called Muong All, somewhere south of Xiangkhouang Province. I adjusted quickly, as I had in the past, to life in a new place. I remember spending time with Pheng and Shoua by a river, where we sat and watched farmers tending their rice paddies. At the river, we tried catching fish and crabs by hand. Catching the little crabs was easy enough, but the colorful fish were very slippery. The best way to catch a fish was to trap one under a rock, but getting it out of the water was still difficult. We had a lot of fun, even if we rarely had anything to show for it.

Vue had a more effective, albeit somewhat dangerous, way to catch fish. One day, Vue, Pheng, and I went to the river. Vue instructed us to move downriver from him, which we did. We hadn't gone very far when Vue yelled, "Get in the water, walk toward the middle, and stay there!" Again, we did as we were told. Standing in the river made me nervous. I remembered stories I had heard about dragons that lived in the deep, murky depths of the river. Careless people near the river risked being kidnapped by a dragon.

When I saw Vue again, he was standing upriver, naked to the waist, holding a rock in one hand and what I learned later was a grenade in the other. He tied the rock to the grenade. Then he pulled the pin from the grenade and threw it into the deepest section of the river. After a pause, a huge explosion lifted a plume of water high into the air. Vue dove in, emerging with a fish in his mouth and one in each of his hands. He tossed the fish on shore, then again dove under. When he came up, he had more fish in his hands.

When dead fish started floating past us, I figured out why Vue had asked Pheng and me to go downriver. I tried grabbing them, but they were slippery, and it was hard for me to hold them.

Nevertheless, I managed to grab a few fish and get them to shore, though perhaps not as many as Vue would have liked.

Soon the cold season set in. Before we went to bed at night, we put bowls of water outside. In the morning, the water would turn to ice, which I loved to see. One morning, I found more than ice when I left the hut. I saw soldiers everywhere, running through the village and rice paddies. Confused and frightened, I ran as fast as I could to our farmland, where my mom and siblings were working. I told them what I had seen, and we all immediately rushed home.

We were soon on the move again, but this time it was different. My mom fried and packed more bags of rice than she ever had before. She also instructed her children not to talk to other villagers because they couldn't be trusted. After my father's assassination, we didn't know friends from enemies.

We left during the night. All around me I heard whispering and chattering, and I couldn't see anything. Afraid and confused, I didn't dare leave my mom and siblings. We walked through mountains, valleys, open land, and forests until daybreak, when we were told to rest. For days and days, we followed the same routine, walking by night and resting by day. We couldn't make fires, and we had only a handful of rice to eat each day. The rule was that you had to follow the person in front of you, never straying. A misstep might mean death by landmine.

Then came a day when we had to march both night and day. The adults gave infants and newborns small doses of opium to keep them quiet so as not to give away our position. One morning, I gathered with a crowd near a large tree, where a crying woman was cradling a newborn wrapped in cloth pressed to her chest. Her husband wept beside her. An elder told the woman, "It's okay. Gently put him by the tree trunk and cover him with leaves." The woman didn't respond. "It's okay," the elder said again. "Gently put him by the tree trunk and cover him with leaves." The woman finally relented and gently placed her now dead son by the tree trunk, then gathered some leaves to cover him, sobbing as she did. As she walked away with her husband, the woman kept repeating, "I can't leave him here. He can't die this way. The ants are going to get him." The newborn had died from an accidental opium overdose, and there was no time to perform a proper burial. Young as I was, I understood the nature of human cruelty then.

At one point, I got so hungry that I blacked out. When I woke up, it was as if I was in a dream, because food was all around me, including chicken and several jars of pickled fish. My sister Yang-houa and some of my older cousins had sneaked into a farmhouse and taken what they could carry. I hated the smell of the pickled fish and couldn't eat it, even though I was starving.

I tried to get used to the harsh jungle, the starvation, and the constant walking. The revolting stench of rotting corpses, from those who hadn't survived this journey, followed me everywhere. The smell was so strong it made me throw up in my mouth several times. I tried holding my nose, but it never worked. And the ants were as unrelenting as the noxious smell. Their bites and stings were excruciating. I hated what has happening to me, but I kept on.

Scared and starving, we walked until one day we were told to stay behind while the group leaders scouted ahead. We waited several days and nights, long enough that some of us set up shelters. We used a parachute that my mother had found for a roof, while others made lean-tos.

To make the days more endurable, we huddled and conversed with other families. Several people said, over and over, "We are running from the Vietnamese." Hearing that repeated, I began to believe that being Hmong meant being killed by the Vietnamese and that we were good, while the Vietnamese were evil.

I also overheard a great deal of discussion about the group leaders who were supposed to cross a river in the area, make contact with people on the other side, and return for the rest of us. It was disheartening to hear that perhaps the group leaders hadn't been successful. Based on what the adults were talking about, though, I felt like our misery, hardship, and hopelessness would be put behind us once we crossed the river.

Over time, I noticed that fewer people were in camp. Feelings of desperation and desolation had taken hold. Many people, as I would later learn, gave up and returned to their villages, turned themselves over to the Laotian government and the Vietnamese, or moved on without us.

When only a few remained, my mom gathered her children together. She told us, "In three days, if the group leaders don't return, we will turn ourselves in. We don't have any food, and we don't want to starve to death." When the third day arrived, the group leaders had still not returned. My mom approached an uncle, my father's oldest brother, whose tent was near our own. I couldn't hear what they were saying, but I knew she was telling him that she was going to turn herself and her children over to the enemy.

We collected our things and headed toward a road near our camp where I sometimes could hear cars and trucks passing by. Though we had camped very close to the road, it was difficult for anyone to spot us through the thick jungle foliage. On the side of the road, we waited for the authorities so we could turn ourselves in. We waited for a very long time, with no sign of them. Then, we were suddenly startled when someone rushed out of the thick bushes behind us. It was the uncle my mother had said goodbye to. He whispered something to my mom, and immediately she started leading us back to camp.

The group leaders had returned. Overwhelmed, my mom

broke down, saying, "*Peb muaj koob moov zoo,*" and "*Fuab tais ntuj saib thiab pab peb,*" meaning, "We've good fortune," and "The creator watches over us and helps us." To me, the best thing about the group leaders returning was the food they brought with them. The adults talked about crossing a river they called Mae Nam Khong, the Thai name for the Mekong River, one of the largest and widest rivers in Asia.

Again, we anxiously waited. From our camp, Mom and Shoua went foraging, hoping to find food. When they returned, they had mushrooms. More than that, they had urgent news. Mom was breathing heavily and looked as if she had seen something terrible. Shaking, she said, "I saw Vietnamese soldiers." She pointed toward where she had been foraging and said, "They're over there, and I think they're headed this way." A scout asked if the soldiers had seen them, but Mom couldn't say if they had.

Immediately we were ordered to move. At a clear stream, I followed the others and jumped in. When I got across, I didn't have a chance to catch my breath before Mom pulled me aside to make room for the rush of people charging up behind me. Then she rolled up my pant legs and my shirt and ripped off the big black leeches that had latched onto my legs and abdomen.

We pressed on, and it wasn't long before we heard sprays of gunfire coming from where we had just been. Everyone panicked and rushed forward. My mom grabbed me by the wrist and yanked me out of the way so I wasn't trampled to death. Quietly, through thick brush and shrubs, Mom, my younger brother Kong, and I made our way toward a small open space. We crouched down, and Mom arranged the brush to cover our tracks. More gunshots rang out, closer this time. Then there was quiet for what felt like a long time, before we heard a voice whisper, "Let's go. Come out. Let's get going."

Everyone gathered and pressed on. We walked through a

thick forest of bamboo, trying not to make too much noise. We hadn't gone far when Mom stepped on a bamboo shoot concealed under a pile of leaves. The bamboo shoot pierced her sandal and tore a hole in her foot. The pain must have been extraordinary. Undaunted, she tore a piece of cloth from her skirt, wrapped it around her foot, and kept walking. Dusk set in and we stopped, now near a mountaintop. We could see the Mekong below, looking like a brown serpent slithering through the lush green jungle. A sense of relief set in, as I imagined that we were finally going to escape the enemy.

Any feelings of anticipation or relief vanished when, after days and nights of waiting, we were still on the mountaintop. I was starving again, and people were desperate for food. We foraged for anything edible, finding only wild berries. The berries kept me from starving to death, but after eating them, I became very constipated. I slept a lot to numb the pain, but uncertainty made it worse.

"Let's go!" It was early in the morning and still dark, and someone was ordering us to leave. I was weak, but I knew I had to go with my family down the mountain toward the river.

At the shoreline, we were told to hide in the brush along the bank until the canoes reached us. From the brush, I could see lights scattered along the other side. I did my best to stay still and quiet, but my constipation had turned to diarrhea, and I had to crawl from the bushes to the shoreline to relieve myself. The pain in my abdomen was excruciating.

Out of the corner of my eye, I saw several canoes emerge from the darkness. I pulled up my pants and ran toward them. Many people were already in the canoes, but I didn't recognize their faces. When I tried pulling myself into a canoe, I couldn't because the canoe was too unsteady and too high out of the water. An elder who I had never met saw me struggling and leaned over. He grabbed me under my arms, pulled me in, and wrapped an arm around me. Wrapped in his other arm was another child. I was so eager to cross the river to safety, I didn't realize my mother and siblings weren't with me.

People began paddling, and soon we were in the middle of the river. I heard gunshots far away, then more that sounded closer. Bullet tracings streaked through the dark sky. When the canoe abruptly stopped on the far shore, people leaped overboard and the canoes wobbled wildly in the current. The same man who had helped me into the canoe helped me out of it, picking me up and placing me in the water. Then he took me and another child by the hands and walked with us out of the river. Nobody said a word as we made our way from the shoreline to hide in some nearby bushes, the sounds of gunshots echoing across the water and bullet tracings crisscrossing through the darkness all around us.

PART II

Kites in a Hurricane

If you can't fly then run, if you can't run then walk, if you can't walk then crawl, but whatever you do you have to keep moving forward.

—Martin Luther King Jr.

4

Having crossed the Mekong River from Laos into Thailand just south of Vientiane, the capital of Laos, we had reached safety. Yet we were kites in a hurricane. I had not found anything close to comfort or solace. Lying on my back on a thin bamboo mat inside a small metal shed, I felt loss and a growing indifference. Alone and unsure where my mom or siblings were, starving and exhausted, I didn't fully grasp what had happened to me and my relatives, and I didn't know what my future held or bother to give it much thought.

One morning I found myself near the river. The river was brown, wide, and intimidating. At its center were many poles with Thai and Laotian national flags tied to them, fluttering in the breeze. I never learned why they were there. Small boats glided up and down the river at various speeds, while children ran and played in the shallows and along the shoreline as adults washed clothes nearby.

Time went on without much change. I was miserable, more so during the night, when there was little relief from the humidity and a fearful stillness in the air. I slept as much as I could to numb the pain. I prayed a lot as well. Before going to sleep, I prayed that I would wake up in a different world where life had purpose and meaning.

When sleep failed me, I usually sat around watching people go through their routines. I watched them cook, rest, and walk about aimlessly. I watched people talk in groups, and I soon noticed that, like me, they didn't seem happy. There were no signs of joy or hope anywhere.

Then one day, to pass the time, I decided to sit near the front of the shack and stare into the open dirt field that was in front of me. As I did, I saw something extraordinary.

It was Vue, standing in the middle of the dirt field. Beside him were two people I didn't recognize. They moved toward me, looking more like they were floating than walking or running, and they were carrying bamboo and metal containers. All were crying when they entered the metal shack. A young woman I didn't recognize approached and sat next to me. She put her right hand on my head and gently moved it toward my forehead multiple times, crying profusely. I was also crying. Many years later, I learned she was a cousin, one of my uncle's daughters who had fled to Thailand years earlier, and the man with her was her husband. Vue later told me that he was disheartened when he saw how emaciated I looked.

We took our places around the bamboo mat and opened the containers. They were filled with food: steamed white rice and chicken stew with tofu. Spoons and white metal plates with blue trim were passed around. I couldn't remember the last time I had used a spoon and plate. I piled rice, pieces of chicken, and tofu on my plate. The tofu was soft, and the chicken was perfectly cooked. Both had been sprinkled with just the right amount of salt, and the steamed rice was excellent. Prior to this meal, all I remember eating in this place was rice and dried tuna. The dried tuna was new to me, and I didn't like it.

At some point, I fell asleep while the people around me ate and talked. When I woke up, they were gone. I would meet up with them again at our next stop.

Our deliverance from the riverside camp ended up being a big blue truck with a long bed and no cover. On both sides of the bed were wooden benches. When there was nowhere left for people to sit, the truck took off.

We were being moved to an official refugee camp in Thailand, home to others like me who had fled Laos to escape the communists. Though I was starving, I was lucky to be alive. As I would come to understand later, I had survived a retaliatory ethnic persecution, a life of war and unspeakable loss. Almost seven hundred people had started the journey from our homes in Laos. Only around fifty made it to Thailand. Some went back to their villages. Others died of disease and starvation, while a few children died from opium overdoses. Many were shot, and some drowned in the Mekong River.

From the truck, I watched the mountains, forests, and river recede into the distance. Behind me was my old life in Laos. In front of me was a new life that I knew nothing about.

At the refugee camp, two women grabbed me from the truck and led me through a crowd of people. Beside a well, they removed my clothes and poured buckets of fresh water over me. Crying, they shampooed my hair and rubbed soap over my body. One said to me, "Son, oh you poor orphan boy. Why did your parents have to leave you?" The other asked, "What kind of fortune has heaven brought upon you? Your father assassinated, and now your mom and sister drowned." I began to cry, taking in their sorrow. I didn't fully grasp the circumstances, but this was when I learned my mom and my sister Shoua had died crossing the Mekong.

The details of this time are somewhat blurry, but at some point I reunited with my siblings Vue, Pheng, Yanghoua, and Kong, as well as with other relatives. Our new home was called Ban Nong Khai, a refugee camp in Nong Khai, Thailand, a city just south of Vientiane, where we lived among thousands of Hmong and Laotian refugees who had fled to Thailand. We were lucky in that we lived in a large, rectangular concrete building. Our unit

A family photo taken in 1978 at Ban Nong Khai, a refugee camp in Nong Khai, Thailand. In the back, from left, are Vang, Vue, Uncle Blia Pao Lor, cousin Bee, Uncle Nhiachue Lor, cousin Yang, and the husband of one of my cousins. In the front, from left, are a cousin, Pheng, another cousin, Kong, me, and two of my nephews. To the Hmong, the word *nephew* refers to the child of any relative of a person's generation.

had a small cooking area in the center, with a blackened metal cook stand over it, and a bed made from hard wooden boards and bamboo matting. To keep flies and mosquitoes away, a dirty mosquito net covered the bed that Vue, Yanghoua, Pheng, Kong, and I all slept in.

Perhaps the most remarkable thing about my time in the refugee camp is that, while there, I discovered I had another sibling, an older brother named Vang. Vang left the family when we were still living near Long Chieng, had spent a free-spirited life in Vientiane for a while, and then moved to Thailand, where he had been living for the last three years.

Now Vang was about to marry. His future in-laws disapproved of the union, unhappy that their daughter wanted to marry an orphan with no money who had siblings to support and who had lived disreputably. Luckily, one of my uncles agreed to pay the huge cost of the wedding, which would have included a dowry and costs of food and other supplies. Vang put his old life behind him, marrying out of personal and cultural obligations. Because our parents were dead, he had to be a father and mother figure to the rest of us.

I quickly learned my way around camp. For the most part, I could go anywhere I wanted, but two places were off limits. One was near the ponds of brown water that were thought to be inhabited by ghosts. Several people had drowned in the ponds over the years, and it was believed that their spirits haunted the water. The other was near a giant tree, also thought to be haunted. The tree was thought to be inhabited by the spirit of a young woman who had lived in the camp with her mother years earlier. When her mother died, the girl had no one to protect her. Several men in charge of the camp assaulted her, and in her grief, she hanged herself from the giant tree. Afterward, she returned to haunt her assailants. Frightened, they asked a local Buddhist monk for help. The monk recommended that an altar be built by the tree to honor the dead woman and told the men that those who had assaulted her should kneel before the altar and pray for her forgiveness. The monk also said that wooden figures should be made and placed around the altar and tree to remind people of the abhorrent things that humans are capable of doing to one another.

I made a few friends, and camp life became more fun and less lonely. We usually wandered about, running around the buildings and checking out the central market. With all the vendors there, the market had so much to see and smell. We could also scavenge leftover bananas, candies, rice, and other foods. Sometimes, a cousin who owned one of the vending stands that sold *kapoon,* a spicy noodle dish, would pull me aside and give me a bowl of it. I liked *kapoon,* but my favorite thing from the market was a cold coffee. Vendors sold it in a clear plastic bag with a straw, and it was very refreshing. I drank what was left when people threw their bags away, which wasn't much most of the time.

Sometimes at night we played a game called "grandpa and grandma." We simulated getting married and having families, perhaps to replace the family members many of us had lost. There was a girl in camp whom I really wanted to marry. She was thin and beautiful. I never chose her, though. We were of the same clan, and marrying within your own clan was a cultural taboo.

My siblings and I felt the loss of our mother in different ways. Kong, the youngest, developed an interesting routine that required someone to look after him. Every evening, he would come into the house, grab his blanket, and walk away as if he knew exactly where he was going. If I followed him, he would turn and say, "Mommy, she's waiting for me. I'm going to meet Mommy, okay." Then he would walk away saying, "Mommy, I'm coming. I know you are waiting for me," smiling while he spoke. Turning toward the brown ponds, Kong would keep going, but he always stopped before reaching the water and said, "Let's go home. Can you take me home?" When I walked him home, it always seemed as if he had forgotten all about our mother.

Kong repeated another ritual after we had all gone to sleep. He would wake up and in doing so wake everyone up. Then he would stare into empty darkness and say, "I see a cat. It's right there." We would all scan the room for a cat, but we didn't see anything. Yanghoua would then caress Kong, pulling him into her chest until he went to sleep.

Whether Kong could see a cat is a question only he can answer. But I saw things in the dark as well. One night, when everyone was asleep, I stayed awake, the glow of the kerosene light around me. Suddenly, I caught a glimpse of what looked like three shadows in the room. I stared harder, focusing, thinking the shadows would disappear, that they were in my imagination. Yet the shadows remained, kneeling next to me behind the mosquito net.

I focused harder, and the faces of the figures finally appeared. My mom, dad, and sister were kneeling beside me. Mom reached for the mosquito net and lifted it up. I wanted to yell, to wake my siblings, but I couldn't. I felt paralyzed. The three spirits stared at me. Then my mother leaned toward me, raised my shirt, and put her right palm over my heart.

I woke up, gasping for air and panting, feeling my heart race. My chest burned where my mom had touched me, a sensation I had never experienced. My siblings still slept soundly, and the kerosene lantern was still on, but the shadows were gone.

They haven't visited since.

I started school shortly after we arrived in camp. All school instruction was in Thai, probably because we were now living in Thailand and had to learn the language to survive. It was a sink-or-swim approach. Nonetheless, I really enjoyed school because it broke up the lifeless routine I had fallen into, and I felt less lonely around my classmates.

Around forty of us were in one class. Our teacher was an elegant Green Hmong woman wearing a white blouse with a blue or green Laotian skirt. I knew she was Green Hmong because her accent was different from my own as a White Hmong. Green and White are two dialects among the Hmong, with different words for *house, wife, husband, small, rice,* and so forth. The two groups also have different cultural practices for their weddings and funerals. In addition to being taught in an unfamiliar language, many of the concepts we learned in class were completely new to me, such as the days of the week, the Thai alphabet, numbers, Thai greetings and sayings, and simple addition and subtraction. Sy, the smartest, biggest, and meanest kid in class, was put in charge of keeping the rest of us in line. Sy made sure we all kept up good hygiene, that we behaved in class, and that we paid attention. Anybody who didn't risked getting smacked on the hand or the head with a meter stick.

I usually met up with a few boys on the way to school. Though we tussled and horsed around, I tried not to fall down and get my clothes or myself dirty. When we got to school, we lined up, stood for the Thai national anthem, and listened to the headmaster's morning address. Then we shuffled into our classroom. Students sat on long wooden benches lined against long wooden tables arranged in front of chalkboard. I sat near the front of the room close to the chalkboard.

Sy did a hygiene check at the beginning of every school day. One day, as Sy was going around and checking the other kids, I looked at my fingernails and noticed they were a bit long. I hoped Sy would be forgiving, but he whacked me three times across the fingers with his meter stick. Then he looked at my knees, which I had scraped and muddied on my way to school that day. "Run home and wash that off," Sy said. I did, happy that he hadn't hit me again with the meter stick.

On the way home, I took a detour toward one of the fishing ponds, where an old Thai man was fishing. He was sitting at the edge of the pond, splashing the tip of his pole against the water to create small waves and ripples. I thought he was crazy and couldn't understand how he would catch any fish. Then he caught a fish! He tipped his pole in the water again and caught another fish. I was amazed.

I left the pond, then went home to wash my knees. But my stop at the pond had cost me valuable time, and I was late getting back to school. Instead of being disciplined with the meter stick, however, I was told to go outside and kneel in the dirt while holding two big bricks. The bricks felt heavier and heavier every second, and the blazing sunlight was terrible. I felt relieved to get inside the classroom when my punishment was finally over.

When I wasn't in school, I hung around and observed weddings, funerals, and shamanistic ceremonies. Other times, I would sit and listen to harrowing stories people shared about their escapes from Laos. People told stories of others being captured and shot, their bodies thrown into the Mekong River. Stories were told of stepping on landmines and dying or being crippled for life. Others shared tales of people shot while they were crossing the Mekong and of clinging to rubber tubes or plastic buckets to reach Thailand. Tales of children abandoned at the river or left in the forest to die after their parents had been killed were also shared, as were stories of those who had been robbed, raped, and beaten by Thai locals.

One story was about my mother and sister Shoua. On the morning we crossed the Mekong, people, including my mom and sister, had rushed to board the canoes. At some point, the Thai boatmen whispered, "This is the last trip. We're not returning. It's getting too dangerous." Hearing that, everyone panicked, competing to get themselves and their children into the canoes. My mom and Shoua climbed aboard and sat at one end, toward the deepest section of the river. In the chaos, their canoe capsized. When daylight broke, a pair of Laotian fishermen found two dead bodies, an older woman and a young girl—my mom and sister. The others in their canoe had survived.

People had different theories about why my mom and Shoua had died. Some said that my mom had vowed to take a daughter with her to the afterlife in the event she didn't reach Thailand, preferring a daughter to a son because, as my mom had once put it, "Sons are no good. They aren't responsible." Another story went that my mom had kept a lock of my father's hair when he died, and because of that my father would never have allowed my mother to leave Laos. About Shoua, people said that a cousin had given her straps of ammunition to carry, along with a few grenades, the weight of which caused her to drown. According to another rumor, it was me who failed my mom and sister. Had I not been separated from them, some said, they would have survived.

I became numb to the stories after a while. Worse, the horrors I kept hearing ingrained in me a hatred for communists, Laotians, the Vietnamese, and Thais, though I had met or known few of them.

I got nice breaks from boredom and dreary stories when local Thais showed us movies in camp. One movie I particularly remember was *Jesus Christ Superstar.* Another time, Vang took Kong and me to see a movie at a theater in Nong Khai. The movie starred Jackie Chan, whose character pairs up with kung fu spirits to fight bad guys. I thought it was hilarious and full of action. Aside from movies, I enjoyed making a simple, diamond-shaped kite out of plastic and flying it in various open areas. As I observed the kite flying in the endless blue sky, I felt peaceful.

At the end of the school year, we were given several exams to determine where we ranked in class. We didn't know much about the exams, but we knew, or thought we knew, enough to understand that ranking last would mean failure, while coming in first would mean success in life. Up first was the reading test, where we read a few stories and answered questions about them. Next was the writing section, where we had to write about who we were, where we lived, and how to live a responsible life (according to our instructor). Finally, we completed a verbal section, where we had to memorize a short passage and recite it in front of the class. Tests involved a lot of memorization, which I discovered I was pretty good at, although I was still nervous and anxious about my test scores. When I got them back, though, I was ecstatic—I ranked fourth in my class! I was especially proud of myself because all the exams were in Thai.

Shortly after my exams, we moved again. On the bus, I looked through a dirty window to catch a final glimpse of my old school. The building was empty and looked abandoned. The sight reminded me of the bombed-out school my father had shown me.

Many strange villages appeared before the bus windows. Most were located along the road, while others could be seen in the distance, some built on high stilts. Scenic backdrops of lush green rice plantations, as well as mountains and open sky, framed many of the houses. The people intrigued me as well. I saw many women carrying large buckets of water, using a bamboo stick crossed over their neck and shoulders to support buckets on either side of them. I was amazed at how they were able to balance the heavy buckets and still walk quickly and gracefully. There were many Buddhist monks in saffron-colored robes. I saw some walking along the road or in villages. I was equally fascinated by the ornate Buddhist temples.

The new refugee camp was called Ban Vinai, also known as the Ban Vinai Holding Center. It was in Loei Province, about one hundred miles southwest of Nong Khai.

Ban Vinai was a large complex, much larger than the refugee camp near Nong Khai. Yet despite its size, there were already so many refugees in camp that our family had to build our own hut. We built our uncle's hut first, near the bottom of a mountain we called "Roob Vinai." Giving Hmong names such as Roob Vinai, or "Vinai Mountain," to key places we had been was very common. We lived with my uncle and his family of eight until we completed another section on the shelter where we could live.

Shortly after we finished our hut, a cousin from Nong Khai

This family picture was taken in 1979 at Ban Vinai, a refugee camp in Loei, Thailand, as part of the application process for refugee relocation. Pictured from left are Pheng, Vue, Kong, Vang, Vang's wife Bao Lee holding their daughter, me, and Yanghoua.

Uncle Nhiachue with cousins, nephews, and my brother Kong (front, wearing a striped shirt) at Ban Vinai in 1979. Our hut is to the left. I remember playing on this dirt road as a child in the camp.

came with his family to the camp. They stayed with us until they finished their hut, built only a few yards from ours. Our cousin had a wife, four sons, and three daughters. One of the boys was about my age, but I didn't get along with him because he made himself out to be better than me and because he wore good clothes. When we learned other cousins of ours lived in camp, so close that we could see their hut from our doorstep, we tried to get along with them as well, but again they looked down on us. We even had trouble connecting with my mother's siblings, who were living in camp as well. Vue, Pheng, Yanghoua, Kong, and I visited them a few times, but they didn't seem to enjoy our company. They must have thought that because we were orphans, we would end up being more mouths to feed.

Along with the other kids, I roamed around camp a lot, often without any adult supervision. To keep us in line, and to keep us safe, adults told children cautionary tales about what could happen to them if they misbehaved. One story was about a little boy who went looking for his parents, fell into a pit toilet, and drowned. Another story told of a kid who, while hunting birds, got shot in the eye with a rock fired from a slingshot. And then there was the one about a girl whom adults referred to as the "little beauty queen," a young girl whose mother took her to Bangkok and was never seen again. These stories were meant to teach us something, but I never paid them much attention.

Games were an essential part of camp life not only for camaraderie but also as a way to cut through the boredom. We developed several games that became favorites. One was the "ass-kicking game." The rules were simple. First, you could only kick the backside of players who were standing up. Second, you could only kick people in the ass and nowhere else. Third, there was no teaming up. To keep from getting kicked, I seldom stood up. When I did, I was rarely successful, probably because I was too young.

Another popular pastime was a game similar to baseball. Two teams played on a field divided into infield and outfield areas, and the game included hitting, throwing, scoring, getting out, and having a lot of fun. We played with a stick about three feet long that we used to hit another stick, which was about six inches long. The object of the game, like baseball, was to score runs and avoid outs.

Even more than games, the most entertaining thing we did in camp was to listen to stories that elders had brought from Laos to Thailand, stories that had been passed down in the oral tradition from one generation to the next and were among their most prized possessions.

These stories were not like those that adults told children to scare them. Late in the evening, with a lot of energy and enthusiasm, elders told love stories, tragic stories, or funny stories. Some were about epic heroes, giants, flying horses, and magic, while others were about the Hmong migration from China hundreds of years ago. Sometimes the plots and details changed, but the messages never did, and every story still began, "A long, long time ago." Elders loved telling stories, as they were an escape for all of us from the harsh realities of our lives in a Thai refugee camp far from our ancestral homes in Laos.

One story I really liked was about the moon, told by an elder:

> When the moon is in its quarter phase, nobody should ever point at it. If you do, it will slice your ear, causing it to bleed profusely. Now, if you're curious and ever have the courage to point to the quarter moon and get your ear sliced, here are the steps you need to take to heal it. First, immediately spit in your hand and rub it against your ear. Then, as you are rubbing your hand around your ear, say the following: "Oh, I am rubbing chicken crap on my sliced ear. Oh, I am rubbing

chicken crap on my sliced ear." And for the most part, that should heal it.

No one dared point at the quarter moon, so I don't know if there's any truth to that story.

Another story I liked was about a solar eclipse because I had actually seen one. Shortly after we arrived in Ban Vinai, the sky suddenly darkened. People began yelling, "The monsters have eaten the moon!" Grabbing their pots and pans, they started banging them against one another, creating a horrible racket. The noise was supposed to wake up the sun; otherwise, it too was going to be eaten. In the past, if no pots or pans were available, people fired gunshots into the sky to get the sun up.

Another story, called "The Orphan Boy," went like this:

A long, long time ago, there was an orphan boy.

Though Orphan Boy's aunt and uncle took Orphan Boy in, they treated Orphan Boy very badly, making Orphan Boy work very hard and tirelessly, never giving Orphan Boy enough food to eat and never giving Orphan Boy new clothes. And when Orphan Boy got sick, they said Orphan Boy was lazy and pretending. The other villagers, too, weren't very generous to Orphan Boy. To the villagers, Orphan Boy was just a worthless mouth to feed.

Feeling hopeless and helpless, Orphan Boy would weep and wish for Orphan Boy's mother and father to help Orphan Boy. To help Orphan Boy when Orphan Boy was sick. To feed Orphan Boy when Orphan Boy was hungry. And to clothe Orphan Boy when Orphan Boy was cold.

One day, while Orphan Boy was returning from the farm alone after a long day of work, Orphan Boy came upon a mystic lake. Orphan Boy didn't remember seeing the lake there before. Curious, Orphan Boy approached it and stood by its edge.

Then, just as Orphan Boy leaned over and began to gaze into the lake to see how deep it was, a dragon suddenly rose from the bottom of the lake, leaped out of the water, swallowed up Orphan Boy, and dove back into the lake.

The dragon took Orphan Boy to the dragon's kingdom. There, the dragon told Orphan Boy to watch over the dragon's kingdom while the dragon headed to help his brother fight in a war. Though frightened, Orphan Boy obeyed and agreed.

While Orphan Boy waited, Orphan Boy got lonely and cried often.

Hearing Orphan Boy cry, the dragon's daughter, a princess, felt pity for Orphan Boy and came out to keep Orphan Boy company.

Many days passed and Orphan Boy and the princess continued to talk.

One day, the princess told Orphan Boy that her father would soon return, and when he did, her father would ask Orphan Boy what Orphan Boy wanted in return for having watched over her father's kingdom. The princess told Orphan Boy not to ask for her father's riches or wealth, but for Orphan Boy to ask for her father's umbrella and white kitten.

When the dragon returned, the dragon indeed asked Orphan Boy what Orphan Boy wanted for having watched over the dragon's kingdom.

"Anything?" Orphan Boy asked the dragon.

"Yes, anything," the dragon replied.

With that, Orphan Boy asked for the dragon's umbrella and white kitten. The dragon became very angry, but true to his word, the dragon gave Orphan Boy what Orphan Boy had asked for. Then the dragon took Orphan Boy, the umbrella, and the white kitten to the surface and ordered Orphan Boy to return to Orphan Boy's village.

On his way home, Orphan Boy was disappointed for not having asked for money and riches.

That night, Orphan Boy went to bed feeling sad.

But when Orphan Boy woke up the next morning, Orphan Boy discovered that the umbrella had turned into a beautiful home, and that the white kitten had turned into a beautiful and generous wife. His wife asked Orphan Boy to forgive the villagers and his relatives for their misdeeds, which Orphan Boy did.

And then Orphan Boy and his wife lived happily ever after.

I didn't realize at the time, but the Orphan Boy tale was in many ways mirroring my own and would come to greatly define my future as well.

Another story, about a wife and husband, was scary and funny at the same time. The husband goes away on a long business trip. When he finally returns late one night, he goes to bed with his wife, not knowing she had died months ago. He quickly realizes that his wife is a zombie and has to get away from her.

One night, I went to bed very late after listening to stories well into the evening. As I was about to go to sleep, I heard Vang come home. His wife was angry with him and they argued, and from the sound of Vang's slurred speech, I could tell he was very drunk. Vang had come home drunk many times recently. He had become a pupil of a "drunken spiritual healer," and drinking was part of his spiritual practice. Vang was instructed to constantly feed the drunken spirits that had become part of him. If he didn't, they would leave his body, and he would lose his special powers. Other "spiritual masters" told their pupils that special powers could be obtained by murdering a family member. These special powers included the ability to send spirits to harm others and to protect oneself from knives and bullets.

The morning after Vang came home drunk, my aunts took Yanghoua, Pheng, and me to pick cotton. The cotton field was so large that I didn't understand how so much cotton could ever be picked. After a day of work, I earned ten baht, which at the time was equivalent to around fifty cents. I picked cotton several more times after that, earning about thirty baht altogether. I had no experience with money and no idea what to do with it, so I gave it to an aunt for safekeeping.

5

If games and stories were what I liked best about life in Ban Vinai, then funerals were what I liked least. I hated the noise of the drum and the *qeej*. Even worse were the weeping and grieving people. The rank smell of decomposing bodies filled the thick air, the stench foul enough to make me nauseous. A few times, I went to the burial sites, which weren't too far from where everyone lived. Adults usually kept children away from the burials, but death was so common that funeral processions became normal. The dead were usually buried three days or sometimes longer after they died, their reeking corpses dressed in traditional Hmong clothes brought through public spaces for all to see.

One good thing to come out of all the death and sorrow was music. With heavy hearts and little to do, many Hmong adults and adolescents taught themselves to play various instruments, including the guitar and drums. They wrote songs, and later they learned to use microphones and video cassette players to make recordings. Most of the songs were about the loss of their homeland and an ancient way of life. Other songs urged the Hmong to love one another and stay together, while some, in a different vein, protested poverty and the kinds of social injustices and military atrocities that had displaced the Hmong from Laos.

"4-4-6-3-7."

The numbers were spoken in Thai over the loudspeakers positioned on tall poles throughout Ban Vinai. When I heard them, I was very excited, because I knew that series of numbers matched our application for relocation to the United States. It was March 1980, and we had been in Thailand for more than two years.

Many of us quickly came to know America as the "heavenly kingdom above the clouds where cities glittered of gold." To get there, one had to go inside the belly of an "iron eagle." Suffering was thought to disappear in America, where a person would be provided an education and opportunities to succeed, something that I and most of my friends couldn't comprehend.

We were going to America because Vang's mother-in-law had agreed to sponsor us: Vang, his wife, their daughter, my four other siblings, and me. She had immigrated to the United States years earlier, one of the first Hmong refugees to do so. Her family was one of many Hmong families to have worked closely with the United States during the Secret War, so she was given preferential treatment.

Before we left, our uncles held a *baci* ceremony to bless our journey, to ask good spirits and our ancestors to grant us safe passage and prosperity in a foreign land. Many families attended the ceremony, tying strings around our wrists and wishing us good luck. During the ceremony, I overheard several elders mention another ceremony that my uncles had performed several months back, one to free my parents' spirits from the world between reality and the world of our ancestors so they could reincarnate.

For more than two years, whenever I was around family or at a social event, I had heard stories about America. One was that Americans were all tall and blond and would welcome Hmong refugees with open arms. Another was that America was a place of giants who ate people.

As the day we were scheduled to leave approached, my aunt returned the thirty baht I had given her to save. I took the money, and a few of my friends and I went to the market near the center of camp. I bought my favorite, the coffee drink sold in plastic bags. I also bought bubble gum that had pictures of Mu Diam

I wore my best American clothes on the day in 1980 when we left Ban Vinai for Bangkok, a couple weeks before flying to the United States. From left to right are Kong, me, Pheng, and Yanghoua.

(the masked green hornet) on the package, along with some new clothes, which I had never owned before. It was a pair of burgundy dress shoes, gray dress pants, and a dark red shirt with a gold dragon on its front. I thought I looked great in my new clothes and liked them a lot.

On the day we left, many people crowded around the buses. People said their goodbyes, and I heard more than one person say, "*Nej mus zoo mog; mus es sib hlub os mog. Peb tsis paub xyov peb puas tau sib ntsib dhua lawm os mog.*" ("Best wishes to you. Take care and love each other. We don't know if we'll ever see each other again.") Their words made me very sad, and I turned away.

Then the bus lurched forward and we were on our way to Bangkok. When we got there, we entered a compound surrounded by a very high concrete wall. Behind it, I was housed with my siblings, sister-in-law, and niece in a concrete, square room. We had to sleep on a thin bamboo sheet, but the room had electricity and accessible water. There we waited for many days, not knowing what would come next or when we would finally set off for America. Many times, I stared at the high concrete wall and wondered what was beyond it.

The day leading up to our departure from Thailand was exhausting. Not knowing where I was or where I was going, I was taken from one place to another by people I had never met. When we were at last on a plane, I was shown to my seat, then I quickly fell asleep.

When the plane landed in Hong Kong, we deboarded and spent the night in a hotel in the huge city. On the way to the hotel, I heard strange noises and saw tall buildings, huge crowds of people, and vehicles such as cars and motorcycles, all for the first time. That was the first night I slept on a mattress, and it was strange and uncomfortable. The next morning, we ate steamed buns for breakfast—which I wasn't fond of—before returning to the airport later in the day.

On the next plane, I went through another long cycle of sleeping and waking up. Eventually, a flight attendant gestured for me, my five siblings, my sister-in-law, and my niece to leave our seats. I didn't feel any relief or excitement. Instead, I felt numb, all my hope and energy spent. But everyone was leaving, and I willed myself to follow, to get off the plane, down the jet bridge, and into another waiting room.

At some point, the waiting became too much for me. I had been doing it for years. I became disoriented and, for the first time, completely deflated. Over nearly three years, I had endured leaving my home in Pakay, my father's assassination, the long overland journey to the Mekong River, the deaths of my mother and sister, and harsh living conditions in refugee camps. Now, just off a plane that had, unbeknownst to me, brought me and my family halfway around the world, I wanted everything to end.

I desperately wanted all the running, confusion, suffering, and hopelessness to finally end.

Relief came when two Hmong men arrived to take us from the airport in Los Angeles, California. One looked like he was in his early twenties, and the other looked older, perhaps in his thirties. Walking through the airport, I could see many planes parked near the terminal or moving over the huge tarmac. It was my first time seeing a plane in daylight. I had little understanding of what it was other than that it would take us to America.

The sun was bright when we left the airport. A cool breeze quickly went through my thin clothes. All around me, there were cars. They were everywhere, more than I had ever seen in my life. We walked through row after row of cars before stopping next to a white one. The younger man put our bags in the trunk and told us to get in the backseat. I was excited, as I had never been in a car with huge bucket seats and a soft interior.

The highway, the skyline, the cars, buildings, and homes that I could see through the window all fascinated me. I tried to take everything in, even the sky and landscape in the distance. I was caught up in what I was seeing when the car stopped and we were told to get out. We were in the middle of a building complex, similar to the refugee camps in Thailand, but also very different in that the buildings had many doors and windows.

I was shocked when we went inside one of the buildings. Inside were many people and things I had never seen before, including a television, sofa, sink, and carpet on the floor. I sat on the sofa, which felt too soft. I preferred the floor, where the other children sat watching a black-and-white television show. I watched, awestruck by the moving and talking cartoon mouse in *Mighty Mouse*. It was only when someone said, "Let's eat!" that I took my eyes away.

More food was on the table than I had ever seen in one place.

Bowls and bowls of rice, cooked chicken with tofu, fried chicken, fried pork, salad, and stir-fried mixed greens. When we finished eating, we left the apartment and headed for Vang's mother-in-law's home. A middle-aged American woman accompanied us, explaining in Hmong what we should expect from our new life in Long Beach, California. She told us we had to wear underwear, socks, and shoes, and that we were expected to brush our teeth, wash our faces, and take good care of ourselves, along with other life lessons. Frankly, I was glad when we arrived and the woman stopped talking. It was one of the few times when I wished she had spoken English and not Hmong. I found out I was not a good listener when people start spilling life lessons and instructions.

Vang's mother-in-law was a large woman. She had an odd look on her face, and she slurred her speech when she spoke and wobbled when she walked. I learned later that she had been permanently injured in a serious car accident. Her apartment was not nice by some standards. It had no sofa or television, and no chairs. In the kitchen was only a small white stove and a few cabinets, along with a pile of large black trash bags. The bedrooms had no beds, just a few sheets spread on the floor and a handful of blankets. Regardless, the place felt like home, an improvement over the bamboo mats and the dirty concrete floors I had slept on for years in Thailand. We had electricity, running water, a stove, toilet, and good dishes. I felt like America was every bit the heavenly kingdom above the clouds that it was rumored to be.

A day or so after we settled in, Vue and Yanghoua took money they had been given and went to a local thrift store to buy us clothes. Later that day, the middle-aged American woman returned to check on us. When we showed her the underwear that Vue and Yanghoua had purchased, she laughed. "Those are for swimming," she told us. Unfazed, I wore them anyway, figuring nobody would find out.

Eleven of us lived in that small apartment, but it never felt crowded. We were rarely all together during the day. At night, Vang's mother-in-law and her two children, Boom and Kaying, took one of the bedrooms, Vang and his family slept in the other bedroom, and the rest of us slept in the living room. I learned later that we weren't living like other Hmong refugees with American sponsors. Many Hmong refugees had more resources, such as new clothes, shoes, beds, furniture, toys, televisions, and even sweet things to eat. Yet I had nothing but confidence in our host. She had been in America for several years, so I figured she must have mastered what I eventually learned was the "American way." I figured if I ever ran into problems or trouble, she would be there to help.

Of the many things that excited me about being in America, going to school wasn't one of them. I hadn't forgotten about testing fourth in my class at the refugee camp, but I also hadn't forgotten about the destroyed school my father had shown me in Laos.

Taking a bus to school was a new experience for me. I didn't like it and was comforted only by the fact that Pheng was with me. The school itself was intimidating, as were the other students. The class had a mixture of Black, Brown, and White students but none that looked like Pheng and me. A woman in a blue dress, whose name I never learned, greeted us when we got off the bus. She took us to an office in the school, where another woman sitting behind a desk gestured for us to take a seat. Several people then approached and greeted us. Then Pheng and I were separated. I was taken by the hand and walked through the school, up a flight of stairs and into a classroom. The teacher introduced me to the other second graders. I sat by the other kids in a big circle, and the teacher continued her lesson. She held up a card, said what color it was, and the class repeated what she had said—none of which I understood.

The teacher continued until the other students suddenly got up and started for the door. I followed, not knowing they were heading outside for recess. I had no idea what I was supposed to do, so I stood by the doors and watched. The other kids played on the asphalt, on the playground, and in a grassy area. They played football, basketball, tag, or just ran around chasing each other. I moved away from the door when I noticed a group of five kids staring at me. I felt scared, not knowing what they were going to do. Then I caught a glimpse of Pheng, who was standing by himself across the playground, leaning against a wall. Since Pheng was a lot bigger than any of the kids glaring at me, I figured I would be safer near him if anything happened. Pheng and I stood side by side, not saying anything to each other as we watched the other kids play. That we were out of our element is an understatement.

When the bell rang, everyone stopped what they were doing and started for the doors. I did the same, joining the end of the line. Pheng went ahead of me to join his line, and without him by my side, the five kids who had been eyeballing me saw their opportunity to pounce. They started pushing and shoving me, then punching me. Eventually, one of them grabbed me and threw me to the ground. I knew I had to do something quick, so I started crying as loud as I could. An adult heard me and intervened before the kids had a chance to do any more damage.

More than colors or my ABCs, I learned during my first day of school that America wasn't so different from Laos or Thailand in an important regard—that I needed to develop a new set of skills in order to survive.

Sometime after my first day of school, Vang's mother-in-law showed us another part of what it took to make it in our new world. With Yanghoua, Pheng, Kong, and me in tow, she went about her morning routine of collecting aluminum cans for resale. She pushed a metal shopping cart in which she stacked black trash bags filled with cans. Block by block she went, checking trash bins for cans. When she found leftover food or a nearly empty bottle of soda, she tossed them aside. We drank the leftover soda, which wasn't so bad and tasted like sodas I had had in Thailand. When we returned home late in the evening, we had five bags of cans. We removed the cans from the bags and crushed them with our feet. Then we returned the crushed cans to trash bags, ending up with about a bag and a half full of crushed cans.

The next morning, we went rummaging for cans again. A week later, we had stacked bags of crushed cans from floor to ceiling in the kitchen. The bags began to smell and maggots started to make their way onto the kitchen floor. Even so, I didn't mind the scavenging, as I liked some of the food people had thrown away. Two men eventually came to the apartment and took the bags of crushed cans away. I overhead Vang, his wife, and his mother-in-law talking about the cans, discussing how Vang's mother-in-law had made three to four hundred dollars from selling them. Vang's mother-in-law, however, didn't get to keep the money. Another family member kept it for her because of her impairments. I never thought less of Vang's mother-in-law because of her difficulties, and I eventually started to look at her as a mother figure.

In addition to going to school during the weekdays, I went to church on Sundays. I don't recall its denomination, though the church itself intrigued me at first, with its large doors and high ceiling. But sitting in the pew each week quickly become something I didn't look forward to. I didn't enjoy church because I couldn't understand what was being said. English still sounded to me like a collection of hissing sounds. When church ended, I always made sure to exit as quickly as I could. I dashed outside, beating the bushes around the church in search of red berries, grabbing handfuls to take home.

Sometime later, I went to a large office building with many windows. I remember the day well because it was my birthday, my first birthday in a sense because it was the first time anyone had ever told me how old I was. When I got to the office, someone excitedly told me, "Happy birthday!" and held up eight fingers to my face. I didn't feel much excitement, as I didn't understand what my birthday meant or why it deserved celebrating. A few days later, during a visit to a different office where a social worker asked us how we were doing, I learned that I was born on April 5, 1972. I also learned that day, from the woman who had first accompanied us when we arrived in California, that I needed to memorize my home phone number, the name of the city where I lived, and my address, presumably because she thought it was important for us to have that information handy.

In having to do this, the cognitive patterns that I had learned in Laos were disrupted. The challenges of hunting, farming, living in remote villages away from the outside world, running from the Pathet Lao and the Vietnamese, surviving refugee camp life, and honoring our ancient cultural practices all suddenly seemed irrelevant.

When the weather got hot, school let out for the summer. I spent my days hanging out with three Hmong kids from my home and neighborhood: Skinny, Boom, and Boom's younger half-sister, Kaying. Boom was strong and fast. While his mother was Hmong, his father was Thai. Skinny was the oldest and usually took the lead. Kaying was a few years younger than us and had a reserved personality. The four of us played marbles, walked around the neighborhood, went to a nearby park, or explored the woods and river near our apartment. We seldom saw Americans with white skin, to the degree that I sometimes thought I couldn't be in America. Also, I worried that maybe the rumors I had heard in the Thai camps were true, that it was only a matter of time before giants would gobble us up.

When we weren't roaming around, we spent a lot of time playing in the dirt field adjacent to Skinny's apartment. Eventually, I got to know Skinny's parents well. His mom never approved of us goofing around or playing silly games, and his father felt the same way. When they caught us playing marbles, they would yell, "What are you children doing? Don't you have better things to do? You little maggots, go find something better to do!" We feared Skinny's parents, but like most kids, we didn't listen.

One time, however, we went too far, and Skinny's mother finally had to resort to stronger tactics to prevent us from misbehaving. Skinny, Boom, and I came across a small garden in front of an apartment complex. Unable to ignore the garden, we plucked all the sprouts from it. We had a great time, throwing handfuls of sprouts and dirt against a brick wall and at each other. When we had had our fun, we went on our way, unaware of what waited for us when we returned to Skinny's. When we did, Skinny's mom was standing in the doorway. Her menacing glare said it all: Come here, you three.

I knew I was in trouble when I saw his mom's rage. She pulled out a long, flat meter stick she had hidden behind her back. For a moment, I thought about running away, but something told me I wouldn't make it. "Bend down now!" Skinny's mom ordered. We obliged without any question, getting in line, Boom first, then Skinny, then me. When Skinny's mom started to slap our backsides with the meter stick, she asked repeatedly, "Are you going to do it again?" "No!" we groaned. After the seventh or eighth time Skinny's mom hit me, I couldn't take it anymore. I started crying, then peeked up at her to make certain she saw my tears. It worked, because Skinny's mom told me to get up and leave, pointing her stick at the sidewalk. I walked away and didn't look back.

Another time, when I was the one who was guilty of violence, hurting someone brought me more regret than satisfaction.

Walking home alone from Skinny's, I caught sight of one of the kids who had jumped me during my first day of school. He was playing in a sandbox with several yellow trucks, unaware of my presence. Then I was going toward him, led on by an anger that I couldn't control. When the kid saw me coming, he stood up. I jumped and kicked him in the chest. When he fell, I put my right foot on his chest, pressing him to the ground. As the boy who had harmed me for no reason writhed helplessly beneath my foot, our eyes met. I glared at him, mustering all the disgust I could into my face. Then I realized the boy was having a hard time breathing and that his face had gone pale. There was fear in his eyes, and I picked up on his helplessness, a feeling I knew all too well. Immediately, I lifted my foot up and turned away.

I ran as fast I could toward my apartment, unable to look over my shoulder out of shame for what I had done.

6

During several months living with Vang's mother-in-law, I thought my days of moving around were over. Of course, I was wrong. In late August 1980, five months after we had left Thailand for Long Beach, I was playing in an alley near the apartment complex with Kaying and Boom when Vue came up. He told me that it was time again for us to move. We quickly packed our stuff, which for me amounted to only a handful of shirts, a few pairs of pants, some socks and underwear, a toothbrush, and a washcloth.

When a middle-aged man arrived at the apartment, he accompanied us to his car and told us to put our things in the trunk. We drove to the bus station, where many long, blue buses were parked. Vue, Yanghoua, Kong, and I were put on a bus, separated from Pheng, Vang, and Vang's family. I didn't know why they decided to stay behind.

Then we took our seats, and the bus left the station.

It wasn't long before the bus stopped at a busy terminal in Los Angeles. People and cars were everywhere, headed in every direction. The day was hot and sunny, and it was warm in the waiting area where we sat after leaving the bus. Beyond the big, rectangular windows all around us, I could see a tall skyscraper in the distance. The tower made of glass was amazing to me, and I starred at it with awe.

Vue went off to buy hamburgers, which I had never had before but learned very quickly that I liked a lot. When it was time to board the bus again, we found our seats and settled in. The bus made many stops. Between them, we drove long distances. When night fell, the bus went on, still stopping regularly. I slept, and when I woke up it was daytime again. I watched the world go by, the houses, bridges, streets, and buildings beyond the bus entirely unknown to me. We remained on the bus when it got dark again. In the distance, I often saw the lights from towns and cities, and I wondered more than once, "Is this what the elders meant when they said America was a place where the cities glittered like gold?" Then I would sleep again, as I had done on airplanes and in cars during my journey from Laos to America that seemed to have no end.

The afternoon was bright and sunny when we finally pulled into the bus station in Green Bay, Wisconsin, more than two thousand miles from Long Beach and half a world away from the mountains of northeastern Laos.

We found seats in the terminal while Vue went to make a phone call. When he returned, he told us to gather our bags and wait outside. We stood under the hot sun on an asphalt parking lot, the oppressive heat the last thing I needed to feel after spending more than three days on a bus. A large brown car driven by a Hmong man pulled up. The driver greeted us and told us to put our things in the trunk. As the car went over a huge bridge, I couldn't ignore the wide, brown river below, the Fox River. It reminded me of the Mekong River and what had happened in Laos and Thailand. As my thoughts drifted back to Southeast Asia and what I had left behind there, the car stopped in front of a two-story, baby blue house.

The house was very nice. A white front door opened into a small foyer with brown carpet. Through another door was a living room with many windows—more windows than in any house I had ever been in. Off the living room were two bedrooms, one with glass French doors. There was also a kitchen, dining room, and basement.

We had moved in with an uncle and his family, all of whom had recently arrived in the United States from Thailand. Unlike us, their relocation had been sponsored by a local church, and it showed. My uncle and his family had beds, dressers, sofas, a dining table and chairs, dishes, and a host of other things, including toys. With our arrival, eleven people lived in the house, but it never felt crowded. My uncle and his family slept in one of the bedrooms, while the rest of us slept in the other. Each of us had a small plastic laundry basket where we kept our things.

Shortly after we arrived in Green Bay, I learned that a few Hmong kids lived down the street from my uncle. Most of them were older than me, but we still started hanging out, mostly just wandering the neighborhood together or visiting a nearby park where other Hmong gathered. The park reminded me of Skinny, Boom, and Kaying, whom I had started to miss.

One memorable thing from that first summer in Wisconsin was the day I tried to ride a bicycle. Someone had purchased a bike from a thrift shop in town and was teaching kids to ride it. Within a few days, everyone knew how to ride a bike—except me. I felt disappointed and stupid because I couldn't do it. Every time I got on that bike, I felt paralyzed, afraid I was going to crash and hurt myself. And, to make things worse, even Yanghoua learned to ride.

Soon I was getting ready to go to school again, this time at Tank Elementary in Green Bay. As always, I was nervous but also excited. Preparing for school reminded me of what Hmong elders had preached in Laos, that education was important and the quickest path to wisdom.

I was especially glad that I would be going to school with other Hmong kids, as it was comforting to have people like me in class. At the same time, I learned from an older Hmong student that we would be around Vietnamese and Laotians, which I assumed meant we were going to school with kids whose parents had caused my parents to die. I couldn't understand how such evil people could be in America.

On the first day of school, other Hmong kids led Kong and me to the main office. An elderly woman behind a light green desk pointed toward some chairs, and we sat. Suddenly, a stout woman appeared and introduced herself as the principal. She waved for us to follow her out, and the principal walked Kong to the kindergarten classroom, then took me in the opposite direction. We stopped in front of a door, which a smiling and well-dressed woman opened for us. She was pleasant and made me feel welcome.

I had been enrolled in second grade. I don't know why, but I assume it was because I had spent only a few months in second grade when I lived in Long Beach. Several other Asian students were in the classroom, which made me feel more at ease. The teacher took me to the front of the room and introduced me to the class, saying, "Class, this is Poe." When I heard her call me Pao, which she pronounced as Poe, I became confused. My birth name was Touger. My parents had changed my legal name to Lee Pao when I was very young, and that had been shortened to Pao when I arrived in the United States. But no one had ever called me Pao, not in Long Beach, Thailand, or Laos. Being called Pao didn't bother me, though. I figured the new name was part of coming to America. From that day onward, I would respond to being called my legal name at school, but at home, to my family members, I was still Touger.

After I settled into a routine at school, it dawned on me how little I had compared to other students. It wasn't immediately obvious to me that I had less than other people, but at school that fact was clear. For instance, instead of having a box of crayons with thirty-two or sixty-four crayons in it, I had a box of eight crayons. And when we used paint or glue, I had to cover my desk with a black plastic bag instead of a desk cover with a cool design on it. I hated having less and being different and felt a sense of relief when Vue got me a bigger box of crayons and a proper desk cover.

I quickly became friends with some classmates. I liked Jane, who was tall, clumsy, blond, and kind. Steve and Mike, the twins, were the coolest kids in class, and all the girls wanted to hang out with them. David, one of the few kids smaller than me, was fast and athletic. A boy named Kevin once invited me to play at his house. It was the first time I had been in an American's house, and I was amazed at the number of toys Kevin had, especially Tonka trucks. Finally, there was Justin, the kid I wanted more than anything to be like. Justin's hair was always in place, he wore clean sweaters and nice pants, and more important, he was always pleasant and kind. Of all the students in class, he was the most well-liked by Mrs. Wilford, a wonderful teacher who cared very much for me. There were many good people in class, and no student like Sy to whack me with a meter stick, for which I was very grateful.

A few months into the school year, we decorated the classroom with pictures of turkeys as well as American Indians and Pilgrims. Right before Thanksgiving Day, we learned about the French exploration of Wisconsin in the seventeenth and eighteenth centuries. The fact that the French had been in Wisconsin intrigued me, given that I had heard so much about the French in Southeast Asia. The French seemed to be everywhere!

Before class let out for Thanksgiving break, Mrs. Wilford gave us an interesting assignment. Every student was asked to color a picture of a turkey and enter it in a contest. The winner would be awarded a three-dimensional, colorful paper turkey that hung from the ceiling in our classroom. I really wanted to win, and for three days I worked on coloring my turkey with bright colors, making sure never to go outside the lines.

When class resumed the following week, I was very anxious. Mrs. Wilford instructed us to place our turkeys on the top of our desks, and then we were to go around to all the desks and vote for the best picture. When all the votes had been tallied, Justin's drawing and mine were tied. Mrs. Wilford would cast the final vote. I was on pins and needles waiting for her to speak. When she finally said "Justin," I was devastated, made worse when he looked at me with a "gotcha" smirk.

The fact that I learned to speak a little English quickly helped in school and at home. One day, without thinking about it, I spoke English with my friends and teachers. It helped that I was immersed in the language, hearing it in school, around town, and on television. Yet my English was never polished, never academic. In my native Hmong language, verb tenses don't change, but in English they do, a difference that made it very hard for me to perfect my grammar. As a result, I thought English would never be my best subject.

Regardless of any problems I had with speaking and reading English, I loved almost everything about school. The one thing I didn't like was my time with Mrs. Seidl. Every day for around thirty minutes, Mrs. Seidl, a teacher, would come to class in the late afternoon and take Maying, Huyen, Samphoon, and me to a small room on the second floor. Maying was Hmong, Huyen was Vietnamese, and Samphoon was Laotian. Mrs. Seidl showed us pictures of chairs, desks, lamps, and other things, all while reciting the names of things aloud. One time, she held up a picture of an old man. She asked, "Do you know who this is?" We all shook our heads no. "This is the new president of the United States," Mrs.

Seidl said, holding a picture of Ronald Reagan, who had recently been elected.

When I learned that we were being taken from class because we didn't speak English well, I started to dislike my time with Mrs. Seidl. Knowing that I was different because I couldn't speak English made me feel inferior to the American kids, and I had already experienced enough feelings of inferiority in Laos and Thailand. Wanting to avoid those feelings drove me to try as hard as I could. After several months, I was out of Mrs. Seidl's class, and it felt great. I felt an enormous sense of accomplishment and relief knowing that I was just as capable as my classmates.

I could still be surprised, though. One morning, I woke up and looked out to a world covered in white. We thought salt had fallen from the sky and took several pictures as proof. Soon we learned about snow, and by midday the ground had cleared. When winter set in for good, I had to wear a coat when I went outside. Mine was dark brown with a furry white hood, and I thought it was very stylish. To keep the cold wind off my head, I put the hood up and tied a string tight around my neck to keep it in place. Then, on the way to school one day, a kid laughed at me for what I thought was no reason. A few days later, he finally told me, "You have a girl's coat on!" I felt so foolish. When I got home, I put the coat away and demanded that Vue take me to the thrift shop to get a new one.

In early 1980, we moved again, this time to a duplex not far from where we had been living with my uncle. I finally learned our address: 832 South Maple Avenue in Green Bay. For the first time, we would be living on our own. Vue, who was eighteen and still a high school student, slept in one bedroom, Yanghoua slept in the other, and Kong and I slept on the living room floor. Improperly installed brown carpet speckled with spots of red was spread loosely across the floors. It didn't stretch to the walls and wasn't nailed down, but we didn't know enough to realize how shabby it looked. Additionally, most of the electric outlets were fully exposed and had no covers. I got shocked a few times when I turned on the lights, which was never a good feeling.

In the spring of 1981, Yanghoua got married. I didn't know her husband at the time or attend the wedding, though I can't remember why I didn't. All I knew was that another mother figure had left Kong, though by now he no longer yearned for our mom as he once had.

I enjoyed living in our new home, but I still felt ill at ease at times. At night, I saw strange things, shadowy figures hiding behind the window curtains or standing near the foot of my bed. Flashes streaked across our bedroom walls. The things I saw were not like the spirits of my parents. When I told Vue, he told me not to worry and assured me that they wouldn't harm me.

I always wanted to believe him.

In the summer of 1981, a cousin and his family from Seattle, Washington, moved in with us. We no longer had the duplex on Maple Avenue to ourselves. Once again, eleven people were sharing space in a two-bedroom apartment, with people sleeping on the living room floor, the sofa, and in the bedrooms. They didn't live with us long, though, maybe only a month or so. At that time it was common practice for the Hmong to move around a lot, as many Hmong Americans were still figuring out where to settle.

I enjoyed summer very much. I liked sleeping in late and spending time outside. I was especially fond of Seymour Park, which was about a twenty-minute walk from our duplex. Seymour Park is large, with Ashland Avenue splitting it in two sections. We mainly stayed in the east section, along Maple Avenue. My brothers-in-law, or men from other clans married to my Lor clan cousins, and my brothers often played volleyball and soccer, while I hung around with other Hmong kids playing dodgeball and marbles.

Aside from playing various sports, Hmong families living in Green Bay also gathered at Seymour Park to socialize and let their children play with one another. Like us, these Hmong families had moved to Wisconsin to take advantage of educational opportunities and public assistance programs. Hmong who had relocated to other states were expected to find work immediately, but in Wisconsin, Hmong adults were given job training, and some enrolled in classes at a local technical college, all while receiving much-needed financial benefits.

Later that summer, I had another chance to ride a bike. Someone left a small bike outside the duplex, and I asked Vue if I could ride it. When he said I could, I picked up the bike and sat in the seat, which was very low to the ground. I steadied myself, rocked forward, and tried to pedal, but I couldn't do it. No matter how much I wanted to, I couldn't balance the bike and pedal at the same time. But I wasn't about to quit. Given that I was so low to the ground, I wasn't scared of hurting myself in a fall. I tried again and again to push myself forward until I had enough momentum to get the bike moving. Finally, after many attempts, I figured out how to balance and pedal at the same time. It felt so good to be riding the bike that I didn't want to stop, so I rode up and down the block until well after dark.

I had fun inside the duplex as well. On Friday nights, I stayed up late watching kung fu movies with my family. I learned a lot from those movies, like how I didn't want to be one of the bad guys. I wanted to be a good guy. My favorites were David Chiang, Ti Lung, and Wang Yu. I also liked the kung fu masters, with their long white beards and white hair. They were wise, reserved, and peaceful, and I wanted to be just like them.

As much as I looked forward to Friday nights, I never liked

Sunday mornings. I had to wake up early before an elderly couple would pick us up to take us to church. It was still hard for me to read and understand English, so learning about Jesus Christ and the Bible was difficult and confusing. The crucifixion horrified me, and I preferred to think about the creator or supreme being taught to me by Hmong elders. Toward the end of summer, the pastor at the church moved out of town. When that happened, the elderly couple stopped coming to get us, leaving me free to sleep in and roam the neighborhood instead.

PART III

Permanent Resident Aliens

Don't let what you cannot do interfere with what you can do.
—John Wooden

7

I was reunited with the rest of my family when Pheng, as well as Vang and his family moved to Green Bay in the summer of 1981, about a year after we had been separated. Vang, now with two children, had visited us and liked Green Bay, finding it a more suitable place to raise a family than Long Beach. To make room for all of us, we found a new home at 832 North Chestnut Avenue, one with more bedrooms, an attic, a detached one-car garage, and a fenced-in backyard. There was a small tree with berries in the backyard, as well as a small sandbox. The kitchen was large and often infested with cockroaches. When we turned the kitchen light on late at night, cockroaches usually scattered everywhere, scurrying into wall crevices and cabinets. The bugs made chills run down my spine.

Vang and his family had moved because Vang's relationship with his in-laws had deteriorated to the point that living with them was no longer an option. They did not think Vang was acting like a responsible husband, made worse because my sister-in-law played on their sympathies and went to parties and other events by herself. After we got settled, another cousin and his family moved from Louisville, Kentucky, and stayed with us for a while. I was so accustomed to sharing a small living space with a lot of people that I didn't mind.

When school started in 1981, Pheng was enrolled in Franklin Junior High School (now Franklin Middle School), and Vue went to Green Bay West High School. Kong and I attended Fort Howard

Elementary School, where he would be a first grader and I would be a third grader, or so I thought.

On the first day of school, Vue dropped us off at seven thirty in the morning. We were early, so we played on the playground until other kids showed up. I felt foolish that we had arrived so early, but I didn't say anything. The bell rang, and Kong and I went to the main office, where we found an interpreter waiting for us. The interpreter asked us where we lived, and when I said, "832 North Chestnut Avenue," the interpreter looked perplexed, as though I had lied or made up the address. The interpreter said, "I will stop by after school today to make certain the house number is correct," which I took to mean that the interpreter assumed Kong and I didn't speak English. I didn't care because I knew I was correct. As it turned out, the interpreter was confused because our new house number on Chestnut Avenue was the same as where we had lived on Maple Avenue. The interpreter took me to my class and introduced me to my teacher, Mrs. Siewart. She was stocky, short, and had blond hair. I wasn't the only Hmong person in her class, either. Chong, a Hmong boy who had been at Fort Howard for a couple years, was also there.

At lunch time, Chong and I went outside instead of going to the cafeteria because neither of us had any money. While others ate inside, we scoured the neighborhood, taking apples, plums, or cucumbers where we found them in yards and gardens. It was wrong, but it was what we had to do to find food.

After a few weeks of school, I made another new friend. He went by Dan, but he was Hmong, and his real name was Dao. I envied his American name and wished that I had a similar one. I visited Dan a lot and slept at his house a few times. He was the oldest of eight children, and he still had his parents, which made me even more envious. Dan's parents were always very kind to me and treated me like one of their own. I loved everything about

Dan's family except one of his brothers, who was arrogant and always out to make me feel inferior. On Wednesday evenings, Dan and his siblings took part in a Catholic Church Confraternity of Christian Doctrine class at a local church, which made me think Dan and his family were special because they were becoming more and more like white Americans, while I wasn't.

After school, especially if the weather was nice, I went to Seymour Park. I played with kids my own age on the playground or dodgeball with the older kids. I also played marbles for money. I took very calculated risks, playing only when I thought I had a high probability of winning and avoiding players who I knew would likely beat me. Winning was important, because I used the money to buy breakfast for Kong and me.

One day, I won a few dollars—the most I had ever won. To celebrate, I bought candies and ice cream. Afterward, I walked my bike across the road and started toward Seymour Park. About twenty yards in front of me, a white kid was walking toward me. When he got close, I moved to the grass to give him the sidewalk and because I didn't want any trouble. But he abruptly stepped off the sidewalk and blocked my path, causing me to stop. When I did, he grabbed the handlebars and tried to yank my bike away. I resisted, and he yanked harder, but I held my ground. Then he shoved the bike and me toward the sidewalk, and I landed with the bike on the concrete. My left knee and my left elbow were scraped in the fall. The other kid tried one final time to wrestle my bike away, but I held tight, and he ran off. Without shedding a tear, I got up. I spat saliva on my hands to clean the scrapes. It occurred to me that I might pee on my knee to make it feel better, as some elders had told me that urine was a bacteria killer, but I decided against it.

When I reached Seymour Park, I found my friends. When one of them noticed the scrapes on my knee and elbow, he asked about them. Not wanting to admit that a white kid had tried to steal my bike, I said I had fallen off the bike going over some train tracks. He shrugged, and we kept playing. I didn't want to tell him the truth because I didn't want to escalate the situation. If I had said something, my friends would have gone after the kid who had tried to steal my bike.

After winter break, I learned that at the beginning of the school year I had been placed in second grade instead of third. I don't know why this happened or why it took me so long to realize that I was in second grade again. Regardless, I was determined to do better in school. I wanted to be perfect, to score 100 percent on my tests and write in very neat letters. By the end of the third quarter, in the spring of 1982, my determination had paid off. I transferred out of Mrs. Siewart's second-grade class and into Mrs. Burnett's third-grade class. I was very happy and extremely proud of myself but also nervous because I didn't know what to expect. Things turned out well, though, and I made it through the rest of the year.

Summer came around, and even more Hmong families had moved to Green Bay from California, Minnesota, Texas, Washington, Illinois, and Iowa. Others moved from cities in Wisconsin such as Wausau, Eau Claire, and Milwaukee. Seeing more Hmong people made me feel more comfortable in my surroundings, making everyday life seem safer and more pleasant. My world wasn't as isolated as it had been when we arrived in Green Bay.

That summer, I spent a lot of time with Hmong people at parks across the state, including Seymour and Pamperin Parks in Green Bay and High Cliff State Park in Sherwood. We fished, picnicked, and explored. At Pamperin Park, we fished for carp, which were easy to catch. The carp were huge and tasted delicious. At High Cliff, I enjoyed walking through the trees and driving up the steep road to reach the cliffs.

Near the end of summer, my sister, Yanghoua, and her husband made plans to move to Fresno, California. One day, they packed their belongings into a beat-up 1970s Gran Torino and

A family photo taken in 1982 inside our house on 832 North Chestnut Avenue in Green Bay, after Pheng, Vang, and Vang's family had rejoined us from Long Beach. Pictured, from left to right, are Vue holding one of Vang's daughters, Kong, Pheng, me, Vang holding his other daughter, and Vang's wife, Bao Lee. I was in third grade and ten years old.

A gathering of Lor clan members and relatives for barbequing and fishing in Green Bay, Wisconsin, in the mid-1980s. My brother Kong is saluting and holding a balloon in the back row. I am in the middle row, wearing a V-neck tee shirt.

drove away. I didn't make much of it, as I had grown accustomed to seeing young Hmong women get married and move elsewhere with their husbands. My sister was no exception.

Before school started in the fall of 1982, we moved again, this time to a smaller duplex at 904 North Chestnut Avenue, across the street from where we had lived earlier. Pheng, Vue, Kong, Vang and his family, and I created a lot of noise, but our downstairs neighbors never said anything, perhaps because they were Hmong and understood our situation. We even set up a system with them to help us get phone calls. Our unit didn't have any phone jacks, so we decided to share the phone downstairs. When a phone call came in for one of us, the people downstairs would pull on a long rope that we stretched from their living room to the top of our stairs. We attached a bell to the rope, so whenever someone pulled it, the bell rang, just as a phone would have. The old Hmong saying, "If the Hmong don't help the Hmong, who's going to help the Hmong?" held true.

The start of the 1982 school year was the first time I returned to the same school that I had left the summer before. It was a good feeling, knowing that I wasn't headed into an unfamiliar environment and a classroom full of strangers. Additionally, I felt great that I was put in a legitimate fourth-grade class with other kids my age.

Just as I had done with Chong the year before, I went looking for food during lunchtime. A group of us found only plums at first, but on the third day we came across a garden surrounded by a chain link fence eight feet high. We could see cucumbers through the fence—more than enough to tempt us. A small opening between the fence and ground was large enough for one of us to squeeze through, and I volunteered to do it.

I crawled under the fence without any problems. After grabbing a few cucumbers and shoving them in my pockets, I made my way back toward the fence to sneak out. Then I stopped, startled by a noise. It was a dog, barking and running at me. I ran as fast as I could, reaching the fence and rolling under before the dog could attack me. The dog kept barking as we calmly and quickly walked away.

I started eating hot lunches soon after that, once our enrollment for the free and reduced lunch program had been processed. The school served foods such as pizza, hamburgers, tater tots, and chicken sandwiches. They were all very good and nothing like what I ate at home. I was especially fond of the desserts: carrot cake, brownies, and cookies. Because we had little money and nobody at home prepared lunch for me, I was very happy to have a hot lunch.

Now in fourth grade, I soon learned about the competitive aspects of going to school. In Mrs. Wagner's class, everything was a competition, at least to me. I wanted to be the best behaved and smartest kid in class. Many of my classmates were competitive as well, including Sonny, Charles, Ray, and Robert. Mrs. Wagner fostered competition, putting a huge poster board in front of the class with our names listed in a column on the left and different academic skills listed across the top. When students did something well, they received a red dot next to their name. The name with the most dots beside it was moved to the top of the column.

For example, when a student passed a reading level, they were awarded a red dot. To score red dots, we had to read a story in our anthology, then read it again for understanding and comprehension. Then we had to compile a list of unfamiliar words from the story, define them, and use them in a complete sentence. Finally, we met with Mrs. Wagner, who asked questions about the reading. Students who answered a certain percentage of the questions correctly received a red dot. Mrs. Wagner also awarded red dots according to her "getting caught doing good" system. At the beginning of every week, Mrs. Wagner taped a square sheet of paper on the upper-right corner of our desks. When most of the kids in class were misbehaving, Mrs. Wagner would go around and award stamps to the students who remained on task. I quickly learned that the best times to get these stamps were immediately before recess or immediately after lunch. When the other kids in class behaved badly, I sat quietly and waited for my reward. Stamps could be used to buy candies and other items from Mrs. Wagner, which I tried to do at the end of every week.

The arrival of winter brought boredom. Beyond the occasional visits with family, there wasn't much to do. I couldn't bike around, walk to Seymour Park, or visit friends. Some people went snowmobiling or cross-country skiing, but those were things we couldn't afford. One time, somebody got us a few pairs of old ice skates from the thrift shop and took us skating at Fisk Park. Ice skating wasn't for me, as I couldn't make it around the rink without falling on my tailbone. Worse, the good skaters were white kids and adults, who I badly wanted to be like as they glided around the rink in their new skates.

Hanging out with a large group of cousins and friends eased the boredom. We mostly called one another by nicknames, like Lefty, Greedy, Jokester, or Slim. Each nickname was special, based on traits connected to the individual and a recognition that the person had now been accepted into the group's circle of trust and loyalty. I didn't have a nickname, though I'm not sure why. Maybe I did have one, but my friends never called me by it while they were with me.

By now we had learned that Port Plaza Mall in Green Bay was the place to be for kids our age. The different stores, especially the electronic stores, were really interesting and entertaining because of the shows and movies on the televisions. On the weekends, we would get there late in the morning and stay until early in the evening. We never had any money, though, not even enough to buy a cheeseburger at McDonald's.

When mid-December rolled around, that meant Christmas was on the horizon. We didn't celebrate Christmas at home, but I enjoyed the festivities. I liked Christmas music, exchanging gifts at school, and that people seemed to be nicer during Christmas. However, I did start to worry as the class Christmas party was approaching. I didn't want to be the only kid without a gift to give, but I had no money to buy anything and no idea where I was going to get a present. From that side of things, Christmas was less enjoyable, just as I imagine it is for most people living in poverty and in homes where Christmas has no cultural relevance. Seeing others exchange gifts and enjoy meals with their families and friends made it all the worse.

One Saturday at Port Plaza I was sitting on a couch in an electronics store watching a Star Wars movie that I loved. I was also hoping to play one of the video games when nobody was looking. Out of nowhere, Lefty came by and said, "Hey, you want some of this?" He flashed something in my face then threw it on my lap. It was a pack of pink bubble gum. I was happy to see it but had no idea how Lefty had gotten the gum because I knew he didn't have any money.

Lefty and I had been friends for about six months, and out of our group he was the most capricious. I was close to Lefty as well because he didn't have a father around, just like me, though his father was still alive. Unlike me and most of the Hmong kids I knew, Lefty was an only child. I threw the pack of gum back at him and asked where he had gotten it.

"Just take it," he said. "I got it for you."

He tossed the gum back to me, and I took it. I gave in, popping a piece in my mouth. Lefty smirked and dashed out of the store as though he had something to do. I knew him well enough to know that smirk on his face meant he was up to no good, but I kept watching *Star Wars* anyway. When Lefty returned, he said, "Hey, why don't you come with me?" My instincts told me it wasn't a good idea, but I was curious and followed Lefty out of the electronics store.

Lefty led me to KB Toys. Before we went in, he said, "Just watch me," which made me wonder what he was up to. There were three long aisles in the store, and on each side of the aisles were shelves filled with all kinds of toys. Lefty walked with an easy swagger down one of the aisles, then stopped and looked around. When he knew nobody was watching, Lefty slipped a packet of Flash Gordon cards into his coat pocket. Then, as calmly as he could, he walked back to me, and we went out.

Having never done anything like that before, I was scared. But Lefty looked like he was still enjoying what he had done. I knew stealing was wrong, but I wanted one of the Flash Gordon cards regardless. Lefty knew how to get on my nerves, though, and didn't share with me. We walked back to the electronics store, and I sat down to watch *Star Wars* again. Lefty went on his way. It seemed like he was only gone a few moments when he came back and asked me, "You need something for the Christmas party, right?" I did my best to ignore him because I was upset that he hadn't shared a Flash Gordon card with me, but with no money to buy a gift for the school Christmas party, I was willing to hear him out. My family lived on welfare and food stamps, so buying something extra at Christmas wasn't an option. "Come on," Lefty said. "Let's get you something for Christmas."

I caved in. We went back to KB Toys. I knew before we got there what I wanted: Smurf figurines. *The Smurfs* was one of my favorite television shows, and I knew a figurine would make a good gift. The figurines were kept in wooden crates at the front of the store near the cash register. I could feel the blood pumping hard through my veins as I walked down the aisles, pretending to shop. Then Lefty whispered the plan to me, and I calmed down a little. He wandered off to look at other toys, while I calmly moved toward one of the wooden crates. I moved the different Smurf toys around, making it look like I was searching the crate for something specific. All the while, I kept my eye on the store attendant. Then, when the attendant was helping a customer, I shoved a few Smurfs in my pocket. With Lefty at my side, we walked out as if nothing had happened.

Shoplifting was thrilling. For the next few hours, Lefty and I shoplifted our way through different stores. I only took items that I could conceal in my pockets, my favorite being a small deck of cards. When we finally returned to the electronics store, I felt disappointed that we had stopped stealing. But as I sat for a while, my sense of right and wrong came back to me, and I didn't feel good about what I had done.

But Lefty wasn't finished. He had run out of bubble gum and wanted more, so we walked to an Osco Drug. In the candy aisle, Lefty told me to keep watch. He walked to the gum and pocketed several packs, but not before a store employee at the opposite end of the aisle appeared. He stopped Lefty, and I got scared so I left as quickly as I could. I was so preoccupied thinking about Lefty and what would happen if he told them what I had done, that I wasn't even thinking about getting home, but when I looked up, I was already there. I raced to my bedroom and stashed the stuff I had stolen under my mattress. Then I got in bed and pulled the blanket over my head, not wanting the world to find me. When I woke up, it was dark outside. Immediately, the memories of what I had done came back to me. Frightened and dazed, I stumbled to the living room. Pheng was there, watching television.

"Lefty's mom called wanting to know what happened to you guys at the mall," he said.

"Nothing," I told him.

Pheng didn't press the issue. I was glad, because if he had he would have caught me in a lie, as I wouldn't have known what to tell him. When I went back to bed that night, I didn't realize that the decisions I made that day might define my future. I never wanted to feel the miserable, unforgiving thoughts that came with shoplifting ever again.

I stopped going to Port Plaza Mall after that. Instead, I hung out with Shane, a neighbor who lived a few blocks from me. I heard rumors that Lefty's mother blamed me for her son getting caught shoplifting, but that didn't bother me.

At the school Christmas party, I gave away one of the Smurf figurines. Several months later, I learned that Lefty had moved to Minnesota with his mom shortly after the incident at Osco Drug. I've often wondered what became of him.

In February, I made a new friend in an unusual way. I was playing king of the hill, a common recess game. I was on top of a large snow pile with several friends, while others tried to get near us and take our positions. That's when I saw Roland, an American Indian kid, making his way up the snow pile. As he was about to reach the top, I leaned down and sucker punched him in the nose, sending him tumbling down the snow hill. It was the first time I had punched a person, and it felt good. As Roland wiped blood off his nose, a teacher saw him and took him inside. I thought I was going to get in trouble, but Roland never said anything. Heading back to class, I thought about why I had hit Roland, thinking that perhaps Roland was a rival and that I wanted to show him who was tougher.

After school, Roland and one his friends were waiting for me. Roland wanted to go somewhere and talk about our fight, so we agreed to go to an open gravel area behind a nearby business. Once there, we decided to settle our differences with another fight. My friend Mike and one of Roland's friends stood about twenty feet from us while we fought. We boxed at first, having made a rule prohibiting kicking. I threw a few punches and Roland threw a few punches, with Roland getting the better of me by landing two or three shots on my face. Not knowing what to do, I kicked Roland, hitting him in the thigh and sending snowflakes and gravel into his eyes.

"No kicking," Roland reminded me.

"Then stop," I replied, and he agreed. I was glad because I didn't want to fight. Even better, Roland and I became good friends after that.

I wasn't done fighting, however. A few weeks later, I was on the playground when I saw a fifth grader pushing, shoving, and tripping younger Hmong kids. I felt enraged, the way I had when I kicked that boy in California. When recess ended, we all lined up to go inside. The fifth grader lined up next to me, but not wanting to do anything, I didn't look at him. Suddenly, he reached over and slapped me on the head, knocking my winter hat to the ground. I bent down to grab my hat, then launched at him, blindly punching and kicking. I kept kicking and punching, backing the kid up against a brick wall. Then he grabbed my leg and shoved me backward onto the ground. At that point, a teacher intervened. She took the fifth grader away without saying a word to me, and he never bothered anyone again.

I didn't know it at the time but, like many Hmong students, I was going to get in fights for years to come. I fought back when I was picked on for being different or for not speaking English well, when I was taunted for supposedly eating dogs and cats, and when I was called ethnic slurs.

I met Mark soon after my fight with the fifth grader. Mark's dad was a Cub Scouts leader, and he asked me to join his troop. Of course, I jumped at the chance. It was the first time I had joined an organization or participated in a constructive activity outside of school. Plus, I thought the dark blue uniform with the scout troop unit number stitched on the shoulder was pretty cool.

For the next couple of months, I stayed with the troop, and we did a lot fun and engaging activities. We took a field trip to a local television station, WBAY, and I got to speak my name into a microphone for a morning show. I was so nervous I thought I was going to faint. I memorized the presidents of the United States to earn my citizenship badge, which I was very proud of. I also designed and carved a race car out of a block of wood for the Pinewood Derby competition. I was awarded first prize for my design, but my car performed very poorly on the track because it was too light. And that spring, I wrote a play about going to outer space and meeting aliens. I created the props, designing spaceships and astronauts out of soap bars. Sadly, I never got to perform my play, probably because I lost interest and didn't have the money to support it.

8

Just when I thought I had some stability in my life, the ground shifted beneath me again. In May 1983, with only a little more than a month left in the school year, we moved to the east side of Green Bay to an apartment on Augusta Avenue. This time, only Vue, Kong, and I were moving. Vue later told me that he moved us out with him because he felt we needed a fresh start. He said that so many people living under one roof was not going to be good for Kong and me in the long run.

Even though it was late in the school year, I transferred from Fort Howard to Eisenhower Elementary School. My new teacher was Mr. Aft, my first male teacher. Many of the students at Eisenhower were white, but a few Hmong kids were enrolled there as well, which brought me some relief. The Hmong students were Mong and Bao, who were brother and sister. Coincidentally, Bao was in my class and Mong was in Kong's class. And when I found out that Bao and Mong were living across the street from us, we all gathered each morning and walked to school together.

I stayed competitive in school, especially with Bao. My drive to compete with her stemmed from a natural competitiveness that exists among Hmong clans, as everyone is always keeping track of how everyone else is doing to gauge who has progressed or who has slipped up. In getting to know Bao, I learned that she hadn't adjusted well to life in Wisconsin and that she was having trouble fitting in at school. It was easy to understand why. She didn't speak fluent English, she was uncomfortable in social situations, and she struggled academically and athletically. When we all played various sports, Bao was so awkward that our classmates would laugh at her. Most of the time she would laugh along with them. I felt really bad for her.

When school let out that year, I got almost all As and Bs on my fourth quarter report card. I was very proud of myself and especially of the B I earned in reading, which was a boost to my academic confidence.

When the summer of 1983 arrived, I started spending more time helping my uncle on his two-acre cucumber farm. Many Hmong families took up farming in the Midwest, perhaps most famously in Wausau, Wisconsin, where Hmong workers harvested ginseng.

Cucumber farming was incredibly difficult work. An older cousin would pick me up early in the morning, and we would drive an hour north on Highway 47 toward Shawano, Wisconsin. My uncle's farm was just off the highway. I started my day by bending down repeatedly to clear weeds from the field. When the cucumber field was ready for picking, I had to bend down and search through the needlelike vines and large leaves for cucumbers, especially the smaller ones. After two or three hours of that, I stopped, took off my yellow plastic gloves, and stared at my wrinkled hands.

Farming wasn't all bad, however. I enjoyed hearing my uncle and older cousins tell stories. I also enjoyed meeting other Hmong farmers, who by the early 1980s had realized they could make money farming. And for many elders, farming was the perfect way for them to re-create the agrarian lifestyle they had led in Laos. Still, near the end of summer, I realized I couldn't farm anymore. The work was exhausting, and I was starting to feel my back break down. I had gotten through other days by keeping in mind how important it was to help my clan, but my resolve weakened along with my back. During my last day in the field, I knew I wouldn't return the following year, not caring what other clan members would think of me.

With a few weeks left before school started, Kong, a friend named Fong, and I decided to go hunting in a small forest a few blocks from my house, armed with only a slingshot. Right away, I saw a bird about twenty feet in front of me. The bird was busy pecking at the dirt, so it didn't notice me as I aimed, pulled the pebble back, and released. The bird fell down, flapped its wings, and died. I was really excited. We plucked the feathers and put the bird in my pocket, not wanting anyone to see it. We then made our way to Fong's apartment, where we planned to cook and eat the little bird. But rather than preparing the bird myself, I gave it to Fong so that he would ask his mom to cook it.

When he gave it to her, she asked, "Who got it?"

Before I could say anything, Fong said, "I did."

I was speechless. I couldn't believe Fong had lied. I told Fong that Kong and I needed to go home, glaring at him with disgust. He just shrugged his shoulders. I didn't see Fong again after that, not wanting to be around such a dishonest person.

As more Hmong families moved to Green Bay and the surrounding areas, some of the old cultural clan conflicts were revived. Conflicts between dominant clans often surfaced during marriage negotiations. When wedding negotiations didn't go well, the groom's side of the family would abruptly leave off further discussions and the wedding would be canceled. And when it turned out that the bride decided to join the groom's family, leaving the bride's parents with no choice but to hold the wedding, more acrimony bubbled to the surface. Such conflicts put a lot of strain on the still fragile relationships in the Green Bay Hmong community. Clans fought over which clan would lead the Hmong New Year celebrations and which clan would lead a local Hmong nonprofit organization.

These disagreements resonated through the Hmong community for many years.

My habit of attending different schools continued when, before starting fifth grade in August 1983, we moved to a small one-bedroom unit at 1225 South Chestnut Avenue. We moved to be closer to family, joining an older cousin and his family who lived in the upper unit of the triple. Vang and his family, along with Pheng, lived below them in a larger unit. In our unit, Vue slept in the bedroom, while Kong and I slept on a sofa in the living room. We didn't have pillows, so Kong slept with his head on one of the armrests, and I slept with my head on the other. Thankfully, Kong's feet didn't smell because they were usually right in my face. We shared a blanket, and since we didn't have a dresser, we kept our clothes in a laundry basket in Vue's room. We didn't have a washer or dryer either, so we washed our clothes at a laundromat on the corner of Maple and Shawano Streets. We usually went together on early Sunday mornings when the laundromat wasn't crowded. I went by myself a handful of times. It cost sixty cents to do a load of laundry, which I had if I won money playing marbles.

Moving put us closer to Tank Elementary School, so we re-enrolled there. My teacher's name was Mr. Lass. A few weeks into the new school year, I learned that I had been placed at an incorrect reading level. When the school asked what reading level I was working at the previous year, I said level sixteen. They didn't believe me, because level sixteen was for sixth graders—whereas the previous year I had been in fourth grade. Ultimately, it didn't matter that I really had been reading at a sixth-grade level. I was assigned to level fourteen, which disappointed me at first. However, when I went through the level fourteen readings a second time, I started to understand more of the content, probably because I was less hung up on getting red dots from Mrs. Wagner.

Kong (left), Pheng (right), and I stand in the alley by our house at 1225 South Chestnut Avenue in 1985. I was thirteen years old.

When the first quarter of fifth grade ended, I had started gaining confidence and became more aware of what I was learning. In science, for example, we read a chapter in our book as homework, then Mr. Lass covered what we had read in class. On Fridays we were tested about what we had learned that week. After a few weeks, I understood what was going on.

When Vue and I met with Mr. Lass that November for parent-teacher conferences, Vue and I were shocked when Mr. Lass asked Vue if he had thought about sending me to college. He told us college was something that we should explore and that there was a university nearby. Of course, I didn't know what college was when I was in fifth grade. I was a member of a hill tribe from the mountains of Laos trying to survive in America, and college didn't factor into my thinking at the time.

That year, at school and when I was around the neighborhood, I started hearing more ethnic slurs and seeing racist gestures directed at students of Asian descent. White students would put their fingers next to their eyes and push them upward so they looked slanted. Sometimes taunts were aimed at me, but most of the time they were aimed at Hmong students who were not acclimating well. Even if they didn't understand English, new Hmong students understood what the harmful words and gestures meant. Thai and Laotian people had taunted us in similar ways, but I didn't expect white students to do the same. Why would they make fun of us if they had brought us to America? The hate bothered me, and at times I wanted to say something, but I didn't feel clever or confident enough to use abusive language. Plus, it wasn't my white friends who were doing the taunting. Bullies were guilty of that, probably because they didn't know better.

Shortly after fifth grade ended, I started going to Fort Howard Park with Vang, Vue, and Pheng. One day, I caught a glimpse of Pheng playing volleyball with some adults. I watched him play for a bit, then continued on with my friends as usual. Suddenly, I heard a man's voice repeatedly saying, "Stupid! Come on!" while shouting other negative comments. The man was livid, and I realized that he was yelling at Pheng because Pheng had misplayed the volleyball. Watching that man scream at Pheng made me angry, and I envisioned myself confronting him, but I stayed where I was.

A few weeks later, I was at the park again when I heard people saying, "Fight, there's a fight at the soccer field!" People were throwing punches and kicks, while others ran toward their cars. I assumed they were going to their cars to leave, but I was wrong. They opened their trunks and pulled out all kinds of weapons, including crowbars, baseball bats, and even a samurai sword. Thankfully, by the time they got back to the field the fight was over, and they didn't get a chance to seriously hurt or even kill anyone.

On the way home, Vang, Vue, and Pheng talked about what had happened. Apparently, Vang had been at the center of the brawl, which didn't surprise me. Vang was playing soccer and ended up tackling someone, hurting the other player. When another player saw what Vang had done, he approached him and made the mistake of challenging him to a fight. Vang didn't think twice about what to do next because, he told me, he had a "fighting principle." "When someone wants to fight you," Vang explained, "you hit them before they hit you." He said he learned this when he was drinking and carousing back in Laos and Thailand.

When I got bored with the playground equipment, I started playing basketball. I was a good dribbler and I could shoot, and I was also fast and had good intuition. But the other players were rough and made it hard for me. In fact, when they learned I was an orphan, they nettled me as much as they could. And when they fouled me, they would argue that it wasn't a foul, but if I so much as touched one of them, they would call a foul on me. If I tried to argue, they would say cruel things, such as "What are you going to do? Tell your mommy and daddy about it?" which sometimes brought me to the brink of crying.

I let their torments fester, holding in the misery because I had nobody to talk to about what was happening. But I eventually reached a point where I knew there was no use in staying angry or sad. The best thing to do was keep my composure and do my best. I had learned who I could trust, how to take pride in myself—be it in athletics or academics—and to remind myself: *I will show them someday.*

9

During the summer of 1984, one of our cousins died, the first person to pass away in our family since coming to America. He left behind a wife, four daughters, and five sons. My cousin had been made an orphan when he was eight years old and had hoped to spare his children from a similar fate, but it wasn't meant to be.

I was reluctant to attend the funeral, but Vue insisted. "It's your clan. It's your cousin. It's your cultural obligation to attend. You don't have a choice, and you need to be there for all three days." I walked away without saying anything, but I wanted to tell Vue that I had been seeing images of my father, my mother, the rotting corpse, and other funerals from my past. I feared that telling Vue might make him think I had lost my mind or been possessed by evil spirits. He would have been obliged to hire a shaman to heal me, and he didn't have the money to pay for a pig, cow, goat, chickens, drinks, food, and other things needed for the ceremony.

Early in the morning, Vue and I arrived at a funeral home on Monroe Street. It was very hot and humid, which reminded me of home. Had we still been in Laos, the body would not have been embalmed and would have deteriorated rapidly. Thinking about that made me remember how one of my uncles who had been part of funerary rites in Laos described the experience:

> During many funerals, the stench of decomposing bodies was unbearable and lasted for days. Sometimes the stench

> was so bad that I wanted to puke, especially when I had to stand right next to the body playing the *qeej*. In fact, at times I had to hold in my puke. I even had to swallow it because I didn't want to disrespect the deceased's family. And sometimes, when I had stayed at some of the funerals too long, the stench would actually soak into my clothes and stay with me for days, even after I had washed them multiple times. Having grown up in a world where ghouls and goblins were part of daily life, funerals were always a very scary time for me, even as an adult. As a matter of fact, the thought of evil spirits lurking everywhere pretty much consumed my mind for weeks after a funeral ended. Needless to say, it was unpleasant, but that was the world I was raised in, and I felt a great sense of moral obligation.

More visitors and clan members arrived as the morning went on. I talked with cousins and moved around the funeral home. I tried to go outside as much as possible, unable to listen to the constant banging of the drum hanging near my cousin's body, which was on the floor near his casket. The sharp sounds coming from the *qeej* were also hard to bear. The food was plentiful, though. We had boiled chucks of beef, along with rice and a few vegetable dishes, though I stayed away from those. I was at the funeral home until nearly two thirty in the morning because Vue had to be there late to carry out his duty of keeping track of financial donations.

A few hours later, exhausted and without much rest, I returned. I kept myself busy by goofing around on the front lawn with a few other kids. We were interrupted when mourners carrying dead pigs in plastic buckets and other assorted funeral items started forming groups around us. Then Vue came out and told me to come inside.

My cousins formed two parallel lines extending from the reception area toward the entrance. Then all of them kneeled and put their faces to the floor, out of respect for the special guests who were related to my dead cousin. One by one, the special guests from outside then began their walk toward the casket, led by a person playing the *qeej*. Some special guests bent down and pulled my cousin up. Many people were weeping, some very loudly.

After the fifth or so group had gone through crying and wailing, I became annoyed. The tears, the blowing noses, and the emotions set me on edge. I couldn't stand the sorrow any longer, so I made my way through the crowd and left the funeral home. Relieved, I stood on the front lawn alone. But before long, my sense of cultural obligation returned and I reluctantly went back in.

Then it was lunch. I had made it this far, and I was determined to make it the rest of the way. That sense of acceptance carried me through to a dinner later that evening attended by a lot of people. Afterward, visitors gathered in small groups to chat. Some played cards, while others drank or snuck in a nap. All the while, the women sat in their small designated room, where chairs had been arranged in neat rows. In Hmong culture, gender roles and responsibilities are well defined. At funerals, women related to the deceased usually work in the kitchen, serve food, and stay near the dead.

Visitors began to disperse shortly before midnight, though I couldn't leave. Once again, I had to wait for Vue. I took a seat in the main room, very tired and ready to go home. Next to me sat an elder whom I had seen a few times at other family gatherings. I knew he was related to me, but I didn't know how exactly.

"Do you know who I am?" he asked me.

"No, but I've seen you before," I replied.

"Well, do you know that I knew your dad?"

"No, I didn't know that. How did you know him?"

"I lived in Pakay, just a few houses down from your family. At the time, you were still little, probably about four or five years old. So, how's school going?"

"Good."

"You like it?"

"Yeah, it's okay."

"Did you know that your dad was a great student?"

"No, not really."

"Well, he was a quick learner. Better than most of us. You got a girlfriend yet?"

"No."

"Well, there's a lot of pretty girls in Green Bay. Anyone you like?"

"No, not really."

"So, how you like *teb chaw Ameeka* so far?" he asked, referring to America.

"I don't know. I guess it's all right."

"Well, do well in school."

"Yes, thank you."

I left because I was uncomfortable. My conversation with the man was one of those things that happens and you don't reflect on it until much later in life. I learned later that he was a veteran of the Secret War and was having a difficult time adjusting to life in America. The rumor was that he had fifteen or so children and twenty something grandchildren because he had been married and widowed multiple times.

I slept in on Sunday. Then I returned to the funeral home late in the afternoon because I was told that we weren't going home until after the burial on Monday.

Sunday passed quietly, with fewer people around. By midnight, only clan members were left. I napped here and there through the night, but while I was sleeping, other important panegyric funerary rites were performed. One was *hais xim,* during which my dead cousin, through the voice of a medium, spoke his last words and imparted wisdom to those he had left behind. Between my naps,

I heard that my cousin had told his children not to drink, gamble, use drugs, or commit adultery. He also urged them to be respectful, kind, and generous toward others and to love their clan and community. To me, it sounded like "blah, blah, blah."

We went to the burial site at about ten in the morning. Family members carried my cousin's casket to his gravesite, where the grave had already been dug. The casket was still open, and for the first time I saw my cousin's body. He wore Hmong tribal clothes and his face was pale. His eyes were closed, and he looked peaceful. Yet as much as I cared about my cousin, as much as I wanted to say goodbye to him, I couldn't look at him any longer, and I turned away. Seeing his body brought back old sorrows from years ago, and I couldn't help but shed a few tears.

When September arrived and the school year began, I was excited. My sixth-grade teacher was Mr. Metz. He treated his students with a lot of care, and I came to think of him as a father figure, which I badly needed. In fact, had my father still been alive, he would have been around Mr. Metz's age.

In late October, I went on a class camping trip. I didn't realize it at the time, but the trip was part of our sixth-grade experience. I had never camped before in America, so I looked forward to going. But it was also my first time being away from my family, so I felt some anxiety.

We left on a Friday, loading our things into two long yellow buses. I was so filled with anticipation that the drive went by in a flash. As we unloaded our things, I noticed a group of sixth graders from another school. They were all white, whereas my class included Hispanic, American Indian, African American, and Hmong students.

After checking into our cabin, we walked to the hockey rink. It was still warm, so the field wasn't iced over, but the goals were there. We decided to play soccer, but not having a soccer ball we improvised with a volleyball. We were really enjoying ourselves until some boys from the other school showed up and asked if they could join. I immediately felt racial tension, knowing that anything we did would be "us" versus "them" and that losing wasn't an option.

The game was friendly at first. Nobody was too aggressive and everybody played by the rules. But then things deteriorated. Eventually, the boys from the other school started calling some of us by racist names. The Hmong kids started calling the others "white skin face" and saying, "Let's put them down," in Hmong. The other boys couldn't understand us, of course, but I could tell they knew we were insulting them. Play devolved into a few minor scuffles, and I knew that if we didn't stop, there would be fighting.

Fortunately, a few teachers intervened before that happened. Mr. Metz took us to one end of the field, and the students from the other school went to the opposite end with their teacher. Mr. Metz asked us what happened, and we told him. A few of us cried when we told him about the hurtful names the other students had called us. He calmed us down and explained that we would have to try and work out our differences with the other students because we were going to be around them for three days.

The two groups approached each other at midfield, apologized, and shook hands. As quickly as tensions had escalated, any animosity between us faded just as fast. Our camping trip went well from there. We all hung out together and got along, playing capture the flag, canoeing, rock climbing, and hiking.

After the camping trip, Mr. Metz involved the class in many school-related activities, including a Thanksgiving dinner for our parents, a square dance night, and a Christmas concert. Square dancing was odd, but we really enjoyed it. I wanted to be paired with Marissa, but I ended up with Maria, which was fine. Vue attended the square dance dinner, to which family and friends were invited, and we had a great time. At the Christmas concert, we sang "We Are the World" and other songs to our families in the audience, but nobody from my family showed up.

Hmong New Year in 1984, like every Hmong New Year, was a time to thank our ancestors and good spirits for past successes and to ask them for blessings in the year to come. I had become familiar with New Year rituals, but to me the substance, words, and meanings in them were empty and hollow. The chicken sacrifices, the calling on ancestors, and the lectures were meaningless to me. Being told "Don't gamble," "Don't do drugs," "Don't kill," "Study hard," "Be polite," and "Be humble" didn't register. I often asked myself, "What does any of this have to do with me?"

I started going to the Boys and Girls Club in Green Bay shortly after New Year. Many Hmong kids my age had found that we felt a sense of belonging there, one of the few places we felt accepted. By now, we knew that we were poor and different. We had heard enough from clan elders that we were an oppressed minority, that centuries ago we had fled China to Laos, and more recently fled Laos to Thailand, then from Thailand to America, where we endured racial slurs. From that experience, I started to develop an ingrained sense of inferiority, an unspoken bond I shared with other Hmong children. As an example, prior to joining the Boys and Girls Club, some of us had looked into joining the YMCA. But we couldn't afford it, so we had the perception that the YMCA was for the *tawv dawb,* or "the white skin people."

I had a lot of fun at the Boys and Girls Club. I played basketball, volleyball, table tennis, and various other games. I even won ten thousand dollars in Boys and Girls Club play money in a March Madness college basketball pool, which I used to buy Tootsie Rolls.

Basketball season soon arrived, and my friends and I decided to put a team together. Mr. Metz agreed to be our coach, but he only coached us at school. He wasn't at any of our games, which

Kong and I are dressed up for our first Hmong New Year celebration in Green Bay in the early 1980s. It was my first time wearing a suit.

we played at Green Bay West High School on Saturdays. I wasn't much of a player, and we didn't win many games, but basketball gave us something to do on the weekends. Midway through the basketball season, we participated in a districtwide free throw contest. I represented my school, having made eighteen shots out of twenty-five, but at the contest, I made only fifteen out of twenty-five, which wasn't enough to win.

Wanting to bulk up, I started lifting weights at the Boys and Girls Club in the late spring of 1985. One day, a supervisor came in and told us we had to leave because the weight room had been reserved for team use. As I was leaving, I heard a ball being kicked against a wall and the sounds of people running. I walked around to a different room to see about the noise. A soccer team was practicing indoors. I was intrigued, because I had only seen soccer played outside at local parks. I turned to leave, but as I did, I heard someone say, "Hey, do you want to practice with us? We're short a player."

I was caught off guard. I could have easily shaken my head no and left, but I didn't. Instead, I said yes. For the next hour, we practiced passing and shooting drills. Although I had never played organized soccer before, I was pretty good. I was especially good at scoring, as the goalie couldn't stop many of my shots. When practice ended, I started walking toward the boys' locker room hoping to get out of there as quickly and discreetly as possible. Just as I was opening the door to the locker room, though, one of the coaches shouted, "Hey, wait!"

"How old are you?" he asked me.

"Thirteen," I responded politely.

"Do you want to play soccer?"

"Sure."

"Okay, let me get some information. Follow me." Though I had no idea what was going on, I followed him. Then I gave him my name, address, and telephone number.

"I'll contact you," he said.

"Okay." Without even saying thank you, I left, thinking nothing would come of it. I was very surprised when later in the week the coach called Vue and visited our house. We sat on the green sofa where Kong and I slept, signed some papers, and that was it.

Before he left, the coach asked, "Do you have outdoor cleats?" I told him I didn't.

"What number do you want?" he asked.

"Fourteen," I said. I wanted fourteen because I had seen a great Hmong player wearing it and I wanted to be like him.

"Sorry, that's taken," the coach told me.

"Okay, how about twelve?"

"All right, you got it."

Before the season began, Mr. Kenevan, who was the team manager, picked me up to take me shopping for equipment with the rest of the team. When we got to the store, I was amazed standing in front of the soccer cleats. I had no idea what to pick, so I decided on a pair of plastic Mitre cleats. Then, a week before the season started, Mr. Kenevan visited me again and gave me my uniform. It was bright orange, with my name and the number twelve on the back. I felt an amazing rush when I put it on!

The team I played for was called the Green Bay Warriors, and we practiced at Kennedy Elementary School. Our coach had dark skin and was stocky and well built. Before the season began, we had a preseason match at Kennedy. I was disappointed because we didn't wear our uniforms. As we gathered to see who would start, the coach said, "Pao, you're at right wing." I was thrilled, but having never played in an organized soccer match and still unclear about the rules and strategy, I had no clue what to do.

The match started, and one of my teammates passed me the ball. As a defender rushed toward me, I tapped the ball ahead of him. We both went after it, but I was much faster and got to the

A few of my soccer teammates from the Green Bay Warriors pose for a group photo in 1985 at the Swan Club in De Pere, Wisconsin. Each of us pictured received an individual award. Mine was for sportsmanship.

ball first. I dribbled forward toward the goal line near the corner, then crossed the ball toward the goal. I did this a few more times as the match went on until I was substituted out. When the second half started, the coach told me to take the ball straight at the goal instead of crossing the ball from the corner toward the center as I had been doing. It worked, and I scored a few goals. The success gave me a lot of confidence, and I was really happy that my coach believed in me.

Around the time I started playing soccer with the Warriors, Vue told me that he had found a new place to live and that we were moving again. Vue had gotten married earlier in the year and needed more space because he and his new wife were expecting a baby. I told Vue that I wanted to stay with our cousin and his family so I could finish sixth grade at Tank Elementary. Vue agreed, and my cousin's family even gave me my own room. It was the first time I had had a room to myself, and I liked the feeling of independence that came with having my own space where I could better focus on my homework.

Earlier that year, our class had been involved in a districtwide writing competition. Every student submitted a story, and the student who wrote the winning story would represent the school. My story was about a child who stared into a pond and was sucked into another dimension, similar to the story of Orphan Boy that I had heard in Thailand.

As the school year was winding down, Mr. Metz informed the class that my story had been chosen the winner. I was so happy. I arrived at the district office in downtown Green Bay the following Saturday for the competition. Another Hmong student was there, a girl whose story had also been selected. I knew who she was, as I had heard rumors in the Hmong community about how smart she was. Competing against her and the rest of the students brought out familiar feelings of inferiority. For the contest, we had one hour to write an impromptu story. After I completed mine, I knew right away that I hadn't done well enough to win.

I had better luck at a districtwide athletic competition also held at the end of the school year. I competed in the fifty-meter dash, the hundred-meter dash, the 4 × 100-meter relay, and the running long jump. I won the fifty-meter dash and the running long jump, and our school won the 4 × 100-meter relay. I was most proud of winning the running long jump because I had jumped fourteen feet and three inches.

Win or lose, I found that I loved competing.

As sixth grade ended, I learned I would be going to Washington Junior High in the fall and that most of my classmates were headed to Franklin Junior High. On top of that, I learned that instead of going into seventh grade, I would be going into eighth grade.

Several months earlier, Vue and I had met with Mr. Metz. He told us that it would be a waste of time for me to be in seventh

After I completed sixth grade at Tank Elementary and was approved to skip seventh grade and head to eighth grade at Washington Junior High School, Vue took me to Bay Beach to celebrate. It was 1985, the year I became a Packers fan.

grade because I was already working at a higher level. I hadn't been aware that Mr. Metz thought so much of me, and I hadn't viewed myself as better than my classmates. To get me ready for eighth grade, Mr. Metz had been giving me extra assignments over the last two months.

Mr. Metz's compassion and his belief in me came into my life when I desperately needed it. He brought me hope and good news when I lacked both. Other than perhaps my mom and dad, he was the first person to make me feel that I could do something. I kept it to myself, but I hoped I wouldn't disappoint him.

When sixth grade ended, I moved in with Kong, Vue, and Vue's wife on the east side of Green Bay. Our new address was 308 South Quincy Street. Surprisingly, Vue gave me a room of my own. It wasn't much, just a corner room in the back of our upper duplex, only large enough to fit a twin bed. But it was mine. Kong continued to sleep on the living room sofa, while Vue and my sister-in-law slept in the larger bedroom.

Shortly after that, Vue told me we were going to finally get our green cards. On our way to Milwaukee to finalize our paperwork, we stopped at a photography studio near Port Plaza Mall to get our pictures taken for the applications. When I received my green card in the mail about a month later, it read "permanent resident alien" on one side, which meant that I could remain in America indefinitely. Once we had them, Vue said I could throw away my I-94 form, a three-by-five index card that had my refugee residential information on it.

The return of summer meant that I would have to go back to my uncle's cucumber fields, something I had vowed last year not to do. To avoid that, I took a job at the Hmong Association of Brown County, located on Irwin Street across from Nicolet Elementary School. The job involved stacking fifteen self-adhesive mailing labels together, placing a back and front cover on the packet, then stapling the bundle together.

Three people were assigned to a team, and there were five teams. Teams were awarded bonuses based on production. Xay (who was a brother of one my brothers-in-law), Pheng, and I were put on the same team. Two of us stacked fifteen mailing labels, with the stacks scattered across our rectangular table, while the third person added the front and back cover to each pile and did the stapling. Unlike the other teams, we would wait to put our stacks in the cardboard shipping boxes until the very end of the day. This system allowed us to work quickly, and at the end of almost every week, we were awarded the bonus.

My first check was for more than $170. It was the most money I had ever made, and I immediately cashed the check at a local convenience store, not caring about the service fee. The first thing I did was buy a pair of indoor soccer shoes to go with the outdoor cleats that I already had. They were black, with "Mitre" written in white along the sides. They cost forty or fifty dollars, and after I got them, I no longer felt bad about not having the shoes other kids had.

PART IV

Ghosts of the Past

Let us not look back in anger, nor forward in fear, but around in awareness.

—James Thurber

10

When I wasn't working, I spent most of the summer of 1985 playing competitive soccer throughout the state with the Warriors. We played in Allouez, Green Bay, Menasha, Appleton, and Neenah, with tournaments in Oshkosh, Madison, and Milwaukee. We rode in Mr. Kenevan's huge, lime green station wagon when we went to tournaments, and Mr. Kenevan was always kind enough to pack an extra lunch for me. After a tournament in Madison, we stayed at a hotel off East Washington Avenue. It was my first time staying in a hotel in America. I shared a room with three other players, and we watched television and goofed around. When we had tournaments closer to home, I spent time with teammates at their houses. I really enjoyed riding in air-conditioned cars and staying in air-conditioned homes. I also liked seeing what was inside other people's refrigerators, because usually there was a lot more food than I had at home.

At the end of the season, we took second place in our conference. A banquet followed, where I received an award for sportsmanship. Getting the award was a surprise, but I figured it was because I had been knocked down so many times by other players without complaining. Still, nobody from my family was there to see me get it, just as nobody had come to see me play in games or the tournament. It didn't feel right, as if I were missing something the rest of the players had.

Aside from soccer and work, after school ended in June, I was asked to join a band that a couple of my cousins and their friends had started several years before. Apparently, some of the older

Playing in a band with friends provided some of the best times of my life. Here I am with my guitar at age fourteen or fifteen.

players were leaving and they needed replacements. I chose the drums because I had seen Pheng play them and thought it looked easy. I didn't have any experience playing music, but I had become more interested as I got older. I liked all kinds of music. Style and genre didn't matter to me as much as the sounds, rhythms, and lyrics. I really liked classic rock, especially the Beatles, the Carpenters, the Eagles, the Beach Boys, and Creedence Clearwater Revival. I also liked Madonna, Michael Jackson, Culture Club, Joan Jett and the Blackhearts, Van Halen, Billy Joel, as well as music by Hmong, Indian, Chinese, and Laotian artists.

By midsummer, I started spending time at St. James Park, where I learned that other Hmong my age had started to gather. St. James was closer to my house than Fort Howard, so it was more convenient to go there. One day, I was on my way to St. James with a few friends when a van approached us. Two men waved us over, and being naïve, we went. One of the men asked us, "Do you boys want to make some money?" We had nothing better to do and we were poor, so of course we said yes. The men told us to meet them at the park at around eight the next morning.

We showed up on schedule and so did the men. They told us we were going to sell candy door to door and gave us a script to read to customers. We were supposed to say that we were selling candy to raise money for a summer trip to Six Flags Great America in Gurnee, Illinois. For every box we sold, we would get fifty cents, which was a lot of money to us.

I hated the gig. I wasn't successful and felt like I was begging people to buy candy. Worse, I felt bad about lying. I quit, but a few of my friends stayed on through the summer. I never found out how much money they made or if they ever went to Great America, but in hindsight, the whole thing was very foolish, as we could have been kidnapped or killed.

A few times a week, park supervisors gathered about fifteen Hmong adolescents to form a soccer team and play against teams from other parks. St. James didn't have a soccer field, so we played elsewhere, but we still won almost all our matches. We played our last match against Astor Park, who had so far won all their games. We played well but lost five goals to four. After the match, as we were waiting to get our second-place ribbons, the players on the other team approached me and asked if I played with a different competitive team. When I said I played for the Green Bay Warriors, one of them asked if the Warriors were playing in the youth sixteen league next year.

"Yeah," I said, "and I just turned thirteen back in April, so I'll have to play two years up."

"Do you know you can play another year at youth fourteen?" one of them asked.

"Yes, but I want to move on with my team," I replied.

"You don't have to. We have a youth fourteen team for next year, and we could use a player like you."

I was relieved. I liked playing with the Warriors, but I was afraid of competing with youth sixteen players because I knew most of them would be better than me. "Okay, what do I need to do?" I asked.

"Give me your information, and my dad will contact you. He's the manager."

"Okay." I gave him my information and returned to St. James with my friends.

Later that week, I received a call from James, the team manager and father of the kid I had spoken with. He visited Vue and me, and we completed the paperwork. James assured Vue that he would take care of everything. Afterward, I called Mr. Kenevan and told him that I had joined the Green Bay Rowdies.

One thing I learned playing soccer was that the Hmong community hadn't yet come to value sports or extracurricular activities. Hmong parents were unwilling, perhaps because they were largely unable, to spend money on activities such as soccer. Plus, I grew up being told that sports and similar activities were a waste of time. I would hear, "Why would you get involved with something that could lead to a broken arm or leg?" and "If you get hurt, who will be responsible?"

Some Hmong parents in the community preferred church over sports. Unfortunately, I didn't get along with many of the Hmong kids who went to church regularly. They told me that to practice ancient Hmong traditions was to worship the devil, and that really upset me. I knew it wasn't true, that our ancient traditions were about worshipping good spirits and our ancestors, not Satan, and that we hoped to get to heaven.

When soccer season ended, I started to hang out a few times a week with a group of Hmong girls who lived on the east side of Green Bay. We would go to the pool at Fisk Park or St. James, where we would play volleyball or just hang around. One day, I was about to ride my bike home when a little girl approached me and handed me a letter. To my surprise, she pointed toward the person who had written the letter, a petite girl whom I knew from these outings. I thought she was a very sincere person who had a lot of character, which really made me like her. It was getting dark, so I stashed the letter in my pocket and started for home.

I read the letter that evening. It was one of the happiest moments of my life when I read that she wanted to be my girlfriend.

When I started eighth grade in September 1985 at Washington Junior High, I was still thinking about girls, especially relationships. Over the summer, I had learned that Hmong girls my age were getting married. One day, girls would be hanging around the park or at the mall, and then the next day they were gone. I was confused at first. When I asked my friends what was happening, they told me that some girls were marrying Hmong men in their twenties from out of town or out of state.

I heard of Hmong men my age getting married as well. I learned that one of my childhood friends was getting married in the Ban Vinai Holding Center in Thailand and that his wife was only thirteen years old. I couldn't imagine being married or having kids while I was still in junior high school.

Eventually, I learned why my female friends were marrying so young. One reason was that some girls wanted to avoid an old Hmong cultural stigma that girls were past their prime by age eighteen. Young Hmong girls were also getting married because older Hmong men were promising them a better life. Additionally, some Hmong mothers also tried to find good matches for their daughters.

Given that so much was happening in other Hmong households, I started to feel a void in my life and family history. Without my parents, I felt like I didn't have what other Hmong had, that I had been born out of thin air instead of into a family. My older siblings, though they had done their best, faced their own struggles adjusting to life in a new country. Vang had been attending school at Northeast Wisconsin Technical College, trying to earn his general education equivalency, and wasn't sure how he was going to support his family; Vue was contemplating shifting his religious beliefs; Yanghoua was adjusting to her new life in Fresno, California; Pheng was struggling with his high school academics; and Kong, except when he was in school, was often by himself with little supervision.

When the bell rang during my first morning at Washington Junior High, I followed a crowd of students. I was nervous, struggling not to show it.

I immediately tried to figure out where my homeroom was. I went from one end of the hall to the other, but I couldn't find the right classroom. I did the same thing up and down another hallway. Not wanting to look stupid, I decided to go to the main office. When I asked a receptionist how to get to my homeroom, she replied, "No wonder you're confused. Your homeroom is in one of the trailers in the parking lot behind the school." I had no way to know that, but I thought I was dumb for needing to ask for help. I went through an exit door, beyond which were several long, single-wide trailers in the parking lot. I found the trailer with "114" written above the door and walked inside. Students were sitting around the room, but no one noticed me as I took an empty seat.

We got our class schedules for the year in homeroom. When I saw art, science, language, math, and social studies on my schedule, I thought, "This is going to be a long day and a long year." When the bell rang, I left the trailer and went back inside the school, stopping beside a stairway to figure out my next move. I was alone, while all around me students were talking and walking.

The only thing I could do was go through my day. As it went on and I got through my classes, I calmed down. I knew I would do well in art, math, and social studies, but science and language were going to be a challenge. I could understand only about 60 to 70 percent of what my teachers were saying, which meant that I needed help. Fortunately, I got it from my classmates, most of whom were supportive. I made friends, including Jonathan and Dillon, with whom I would end up playing soccer and who helped me fit in by spreading the word that I was a great soccer player and a cool person to be around.

When mid-quarter grades came out, I got almost all As, with the lone B coming in language, which I expected. The grades boosted my confidence and made me realize that Mr. Metz had been right about me, that I was ready to skip seventh grade.

In the winter of 1986, after more than six months of practicing, our band was ready for our big debut. We had our first gig during Hmong New Year at a tavern in Oshkosh off Highway 21. It was snowing hard that night, but the tavern was crowded. We played three songs, and afterward I stayed near the wall opposite the bar. I was too young to drink, so I people watched instead. A group of five people caught my attention when they walked in. All were well dressed, but I was most taken by an elegant, petite girl wearing a red dress. Eventually, I mustered enough courage to ask her to dance. She agreed. While dancing to a slow song, I asked her name and where she was from.

"Maya," she said. "I'm from Appleton."

"What's your last name?"

"Thor."

It was important to ask her name because in Hmong culture, it's forbidden to marry someone from your own clan.

Out of boredom, I tried out for the basketball team that year. I had never tried out for anything, so I didn't know what to expect. And, aside from playing on a basketball team the year before, I didn't have much experience. I knew I was fast, though, and that I could dribble and shoot. Still, I was surprised when I made the team. That meant I needed proper basketball shoes, which I couldn't afford, so I ended up getting a pair of used Converse high tops from a brother-in-law.

I didn't think I'd get much playing time, but I ended up playing in every game, usually in the second half for a few minutes. I ran up and down the court, rarely touching the ball. Besides scoring a few baskets and grabbing a few steals, I didn't shine playing basketball as I did playing soccer.

New Hmong students from Thailand enrolled at Washington Junior High in March 1986. Because I could speak English well, some of the teachers paired them with me in various classes, including gym. One day, the new Hmong students were playing basketball with the rest of us when other players started fouling them roughly and recklessly. One student, Sam, tripped one of the new Hmong students for no reason and shoved another when he was off balance, sending him hard into the wooden floor. The kid got up and went after Sam, who backed up with his hands in the air and a smirk on his face, as if to say he hadn't done anything wrong.

But the rest of us knew what he had done. Before Sam could turn around, he was on the floor in front of me. One of my Hmong friends had tripped him as Sam was walking backward. I started kicking him as hard as I could, but Sam managed to get up. I ran because Sam was a lot bigger than me. He chased me, but we didn't get far before we encountered our gym teacher, who ordered us against the wall. Class let out, and the gym teacher ordered us to follow him. I listened, but Sam refused. The gym teacher grabbed Sam's long hair and dragged him against a set of bleachers until Sam lost his attitude and agreed to come along.

"These two need to cool down," the gym teacher told a

receptionist when we reached the main office. Sam and I sat, not saying a word to each other, until the bell rang. Then I got up, went to my locker, and headed to my next class with my gym clothes on.

The next day, I was called to the main office shortly after the start of first period. When I got there, Sam was already in the waiting area. Dr. Landis, the principal, called us into his office and asked us to tell him what had happened. I spoke first, and when Dr. Landis asked Sam if what I had said was true, Sam just shrugged his shoulders and said, "Whatever." Then Sam gave his side of the story, which was mostly lies. When I tried to interject, Dr. Landis told me that it was Sam's turn to speak, so I let Sam finish.

When Sam was through talking, Dr. Landis told us, "Don't let this happen again. Understand?" We nodded our heads and left the room.

Over the next few months, Sam and his friends bullied many of the Hmong students at Washington Junior High, both in school and out. At the Boys and Girls Club, one of Sam's friends broke all his knuckles punching one of my friends in the forehead. It didn't surprise me because I had been getting in fights since I lived in California. Fighting was just a part of life for many Hmong people my age.

That spring, I joined the track and field team. I was fast enough to run on the 4 × 100-meter and 4 × 200-meter relay teams. We won several races. I also competed in the running long jump and sometimes the 100- and 200-meter dashes, though I quickly learned that I couldn't jump far enough or run fast enough to compete. Whereas other kids seemed to be getting taller, stronger, and faster, I wasn't.

That May, a cousin visited who had just returned from a year at the University of Wisconsin–Oshkosh. He was one of the first

Hmong students to study there, and he gave me a brochure for a precollege program, telling me I should apply. It was the second time someone had talked to me about college, the first being when Mr. Lass mentioned it to Vue and me.

I completed the application for the UW–Oshkosh precollege program, which helps middle and high school students prepare for college and explore careers. The application was a lot of work. I needed a signature from my counselor at school, along with proof that my family lived in poverty and that nobody in my household had a college degree. Weeks later, I got an acceptance letter.

I took a three-week break from the band and from playing youth fourteen soccer to attend the precollege program that June. I lived on campus for three weeks and took courses with college professors. Yet I still didn't know if college was for me. I continued to think of myself as a hill person from Laos who didn't fit in on a university campus.

When I got back to Green Bay, I rejoined my soccer team. We won most of our games and many tournaments, and I had a lot of fun playing with my teammates, especially an Indian teammate named Raj and an American Indian player named Roger. It was good to have other minorities on the team, as it made me feel like I stood out less for being different.

Before high school started, "Cool Sam" came into my Hmong adolescent world. He was like David Bowie or Steve McQueen to me and my friends, and he made most of the local tough kids look boyish by comparison. Sam was eighteen or nineteen years old and always wore nice clothes, even a sports coat. Plus, he had an American name, which I still wanted. Many Hmong adolescents had given themselves American names. Sheng became Sharon, Mai became Maria, Kia became Katy, Ge became Tony, and Pao became Paul. Ultimately, I never changed mine because one of my grandparents had given me my name, and I wanted to keep it out of respect.

We heard Sam had come from California, where he had been a "gangster," or *yog ib tug miyuam laib.* As a result, his parents had sent him to Green Bay. Like many Hmong parents at the time, they hoped that a change of scenery would help their son, but kids like Sam usually brought their habits with them when they moved from big cities to small towns. While some of my friends picked up Sam's behaviors and started partying and doing drugs, I was content to observe and keep my distance.

By the time Sam came around, many Hmong adolescents had begun to change their attitudes and behaviors, being less reserved and intimidated and more socially outgoing. Lots of Hmong kids traded clothes from the thrift store for fashionable clothes and puffy hair done up with hairspray, all to better fit in and make ourselves more American.

11

We moved again before summer ended, from 308 South Quincy Street to 416 South Webster Avenue. I was glad we did because it meant I could attend Green Bay East High School when school started.

With a week left before I started high school, I went with other family members to Austin Straubel Airport in Green Bay to welcome my uncle, my father's youngest brother, from Thailand. He had lived with us in the refugee camps, and we were looking forward to his arrival. With him in America, our clan would be stronger.

Initially, my uncle had been reluctant to come to America because he had become a clan leader in the refugee camps. In addition, like others his age, my uncle was convinced that General Vang Pao was going to lead another Secret War, one that would lead to victory over the communists and a Hmong return to Laos. My uncle had been a farmer and primary school teacher before the war broke out. When that happened, he ran a fishing business, but he didn't do well. Shortly after escaping to Ban Vinai, he was asked to join the resistance because he was one of the few literate people in camp. Those in the resistance stayed in contact with the Chaofa in Laos and sent funding raised in camp or abroad to support the Chaofa's causes. My uncle accepted the position because it came with benefits his family needed, including better housing. Eventually, he decided to leave Thailand for America when he learned that Ban Vinai was going to close in a few years (it closed in 1992) and because one of my other uncles had begged him to come. He may also have realized that he would probably never go back to Laos.

When we met my uncle and his family at the gate, the reunion was filled with so much happiness, along with crying and hugging. Vue and I dropped them off at the duplex we had rented for them. Vue was my uncle's sponsor, so we had been preparing for months for his arrival. In addition to finding him a place to live, we had asked local businesses and churches to donate furniture, clothes, and money to help my uncle and his family. Vue and I went all over town picking up sofas, dressers, dishes, and other items.

Vue and I continued dropping off supplies and household goods as needed. During my visits, I had a few conversations with my uncle. He was always pleasant and humble. He was also intelligent and had a great sense of humor. When I asked him, "Why didn't you come sooner?" he answered, "Because I hadn't yet realized I was only a cat's-paw!" We shared a good laugh over that.

As I visited more, our conversations grew longer and more in depth. We talked about assimilation and what life was like in America compared to the camps in Thailand. Like many elders, my uncle was quite a storyteller. He was precise and careful with his words, keeping his stories simple and to the point. He was always engaging, and he was especially enthusiastic when telling me about what life had been like in Laos. My uncle also talked about my parents, which I really enjoyed.

Talking with my uncle kindled in me a desire to visit Laos. But when I heard from my uncle about how dangerous it still was, I had no idea if I would ever get there.

A few weeks after my uncle arrived, my family held a shamanistic ceremony at my uncle's house to call the souls of his family to America. It was important to him, and we wanted to make my uncle and his family feel at home in Wisconsin.

Because my parents had died before they could teach me about Hmong ceremonies, I didn't understand everything that went on. The significance of the animal sacrifices, the arrangement of cups and several rice-filled bowls, the burning incense on the shaman's altar, the red veil covering the shaman's face, and the large donut-sized rings on the shaman's hands were largely a mystery to me. Nor did I understand why the shaman went into a trance during the ceremony or why he chanted unfamiliar phrases while a person seated next to him banged a metal gong and methodically burned spiritual paper money.

While that was going on, most of the women were in the kitchen, garage, or basement. Many of them were busy preparing food while the men socialized, drank, or waited for the ritual feast to begin. Once the shamanistic ceremony ended, the feast began, laid out in the basement on two rectangular tables covered with white plastic sheets. Scattered across the tables were various bowls containing rice, hot peppers, boiled pork with green mustard, and fried chicken. At the center of the spread was a huge metal bowl filled with two boiled chickens, boiled eggs, cookies, and fruits.

Most of the elders sat on one side of the table, with the most important guests in the middle. I was told to take a seat on the opposite, less-significant side near the end of the row. Two people sat at each end of the table to direct and monitor the feast and its rituals. The men sat first while the women served the food. I felt bad for my sisters-in-law, aunts, and other women because I thought they were more deserving to sit than I was. I remember thinking that I hoped they would do away with or refuse antiquated gender roles when they became more acclimated to American customs.

Before we started eating, some of the men, including myself, got up and stood in a line near a side table. We kneeled several times, then sat back down. We kneeled to thank the shaman, to thank the man who banged the metal gong, and to thank everyone for coming to the feast.

I decided to hang around after the feast was over. Soon I was alone with my uncle while the women cleaned dishes upstairs. He was dozing on the sofa when I went to a large white cooler and grabbed two cans of Old Style beer. I woke my uncle up, opened a beer, and handed it to him. I opened the other beer for myself. By now, I had been to enough Hmong cultural gatherings that I had done some drinking. I also knew how to ask an elder for a favor that he couldn't refuse.

"What's this?" he asked drowsily.

"Take it, Uncle," I said. "Uncle, if you don't agree with what I'm going to say, you don't have to drink it. In fact, if you disagree with what I'm going to say, then I'll drink your beer for you, okay?"

Since I had followed traditions, my uncle nodded and took a drink. Then I led him to a black metal folding chair at the table and asked him to have a seat, and I quickly took a seat across from him. I drank a mouthful of beer. "Uncle," I said, "here's the reason why I gave you the beer. I'd like you to tell me about my birth and the first few years of my life, because I don't have anyone else to ask. I've heard things from my siblings and other individuals, but only vague facts. But you were there, Uncle, and close to my father, so I would like to hear it from you. But if you don't feel like talking about this, I understand."

My uncle sipped his drink. "My son, Touger, first of all, thank you for the drink. I greatly appreciate it. And, of course, I would love to tell you about your birth and those first few years of your life. That's not a problem. What is it that that you want to know?"

"What can you tell me about the day I was born?"

Although this conversation happened decades ago, I remember my uncle's answers clearly because of how important they were to me as I struggled to find my place in the world. In Hmong culture, family histories and ancestral stories are often passed down through oral storytelling. Each retelling might be slightly different, but the information and values being repeated hold true. In that spirit, what follows might not be a word-for-word transcription of what my uncle told me that day, but I have recorded the conversation as I remember it here as a record of my family's history.

"You were born unexpectedly on a misty morning when the morning dew was welcoming the new dawn," my uncle's story began. "At the time, your parents were living in a small hut in an isolated village on the outskirts of Xiangkhouang Province. I think the village was called Puka. However, only your mother was home because your father was away on a business trip.

"But your mother didn't panic. She had already had several children, so she knew how to stay calm. She already had all the supplies she needed, including a knife, several pieces of cloth, hot water, a warm fire, and a bamboo mat. But as you were about to be delivered, there was a complication. Your head was too big. By the time you arrived, your mother's clothes were soaked in dust and the ground around her looked as though it had been swept many times. You and your mother were fortunate to survive.

"After your mother cleaned you, wrapped you up, and placed you in her bosom, she gathered the placenta and buried it near the wooden beam at the center of your hut. She did that because the center beam is our closest path to heaven. It's also where Satan has his last chance to take you to hell. The center beam is also culturally significant because it's our family's spiritual heart.

"When you die, which I hope will be many years from now, one of your souls will return to your birthplace, gather your placenta—which are your birth clothes—put them on, and join your ancestors and family in heaven. At the same time, you risk getting snatched by Satan and taken to hell."

Then my uncle paused. We simultaneously took another mouthful of beer. As much as I wanted to, I didn't say anything, not wanting to break storytelling traditions. While I waited for my uncle to continue, I thought about the rationale for burying the placenta.

My uncle continued, "Anyway, on the third day after you were born, your parents invited many guests to your soul calling ceremony. To perform the soul calling ceremony, they invited an elder. The soul calling ceremony, as you're probably aware, has been performed for every Hmong child since the dawn of time. It has two critical purposes. The first is to unite your soul with your family, clan, and community. The second is for the invited guests to bless you with a healthy and prosperous life. It is critical to unite your soul with your body because the Hmong believe a person's soul is vulnerable to wandering off, getting lost, or being captured by evil spirits as an infant. If that happens, the child can die shortly after birth or suffer a lingering sickness."

I had to interject. "Uncle, if the soul calling ceremony is so important, why did my parents wait until the third day to do it?"

"Great question, my son Touger. Well, your parents waited because for the first two mornings of your life, your soul was still in limbo between the real world and the spiritual world. Your soul hadn't yet successfully come into the real world."

Then I interrupted him again. "I see. What would have happened if I had died before the soul calling ceremony?"

"Another great question. If that had happened, and I'm glad it didn't, your parents would have conducted a short ritual, buried you without a typical funeral, and moved on without much anguish. Don't be disappointed. In our culture, had you died before the soul calling ceremony, you wouldn't have been considered a complete human being yet."

"How does the soul calling ceremony go?" I asked.

"First, the elder your parents invited begins the ceremony by placing a small round table near the main entrance of your family's hut. You probably don't remember, but your family's hut wasn't much bigger than a two-car garage, so by no means was it as nice as this house. Anyway, then the elder placed a small metal bowl filled with rice on the small round table. Then he placed a couple of burning incense sticks and an uncooked egg near the center of the bowl, with half the egg exposed. Then the elder opened the door, pounded on his gong, and chanted something like this:

> Oh, today is a good day; today is a pure day. I'm here to call Touger's spirit and soul to unite with his body, new family, clan, and community. I'm here to call his soul to unite with his new father, Vayeng, and with his mother, Mrs. Vayeng. Oh, Touger's soul and spirit, now that you've found a family, come and unite with your family. Wherever you may be, in the abyss of the ocean, in the remotest crevices of the mountains, underneath the smallest of pebbles in the rivers, flowing indefinitely in the river streams, gliding along with the moving morning mists, trapped in the dews of the white clouds, or stuck in a moss in the darkest of caves, I'm calling you to come, unite, and stay with your new family, clan, and community. Oh, come and unite with Touger. Come and unite with your new father, mother, brothers, sisters, clan, relatives, and community.

My uncle paused, and we drank again. I thought to myself, "My poor mother." Others usually called her Niam Vayeng or Mrs. Vayeng or by her relationships to other family members, such as sister-in-law Vayeng, Aunt Vayeng, older sister Vayeng, or younger sister Vayeng. I couldn't imagine being my mother. It was as if the moment she got married her identity vanished.

"Then," my uncle went on, "your parents asked the guests to gather around a rectangular dining table in the dining area. Food

My mother, second from the left, with several unidentified Hmong women in an undated photo.

was on the table that had been prepared by your mom and other women, including several bowls of steamed rice and a couple of dishes made from the sacrificed animals.

"The guests took their assigned seats, with the wisest community elders seated on the north side of the table and other guests on the south side. A few of the wiser elders were then asked to perform specific duties. One elder blessed a handful of white strings about six inches long to be tied around your wrists, symbolizing the unity of your spirit and body, and to bring you a healthy and prosperous life. A second elder was asked to do three specific things: to cut the excess string dangling from your wrists, partially burn a few of the excess strings he had cut, and toss the burning strings into a wooden jar half-filled with water. A third elder was asked to take the wooden jar and throw the strings away so to toss away evil. Others then analyzed the boiled chickens to determine if your soul had united with your body. Finally, two individuals sat at each end of the table, presiding over the last phase of the soul calling ceremony that included drinking alcohol to commemorate the event.

"Then your family members gathered near the south side of the big rectangular table. Your mom was there, holding you. Everyone reached their hands forward with their palms down. The elder who held the strings began sweeping his hands back and forth over everyone's hands, chanting something like this:

> Oh, today is a great day; today is a pure day. Today, Vayeng and Mrs. Vayeng have welcomed a new child into their family. I'm not sweeping away good spirits, good blessings, good health, or good fortunes for their newborn or family. I'm sweeping away sickness, darkness, bad fortunes, injustice, and bad deeds. And I'm blessing these strings with good health, fortune, prosperity, and wellness. May Touger live a prosperous life, a rich and healthy life, until he's old and gray.

"Once that was done, the elder took several strings for himself and passed out the rest to the guests. As he was tying a string around your wrist, he chanted something like this:

> Oh, today is a great day; today is a pure day. I'm tying this string of gold and this string of wealth around your wrist to welcome you to your new family and for your soul to be united with your body, your father, your mother, your brothers, and your sisters. Your uncles and aunts as well. Now that you've found a family, be joyful and happy. Don't wander into the lost world. I'm tying this string of gold to bless you with health, wealth, happiness, knowledge, and wisdom. From today onward, may no sickness and illness find you; may you live a fulfilling and healthy life until you are old and gray.

"Other guests gave you similar blessings, tying strings around your parents' and siblings' wrists as well. Then your family reached their hands out again with their palms down. The elder chosen to cut the excess string then chanted something like this:

> I'm not cutting away his spirit or all that is good and glorious. I'm cutting away sicknesses, misfortunes, and bad deeds. I'm cutting away any need to have another shamanistic ceremony or soul calling. I'm cutting away all that's bad and evil.

"After cutting all the excess strings, he partially set a few of them on fire and tossed them into a wooden jar of water. He then passed the jar to the next chosen elder, who took it outside. This elder chanted something like this:

> I'm tossing all the bad deeds, bad spirits, sicknesses, and bad fortunes far away, to the end of the world, the void of the world, to be washed by the oceans and rivers, to drift in the wind to the end of the world, where no ears can hear, where no eyes can see, where no voices can be heard, and where there's no way to return.

"While that was going on outside, the last two chosen elders were simultaneously examining the two boiled chickens to determine whether your spirit had united with your body. They carefully examined the feet, beak, crown, and tongue, then they excitedly concluded, 'Everything looks great! Beautiful feet, beak, crown, and the tongue looks great! His spirit has come home, united with his family, clan, and community.'

"Then the feast began. During the meal, the chosen four individuals, two at each end of the table, informed the guests that there would be two rounds of drinking to commemorate the ceremony. One round was to welcome your spirit. The other was to thank the elder who had performed the ceremony and those who had come to support your family and offer their blessings. Now, how about that?"

"Well, Uncle, that's a fascinating story," I said. "My parents must have really wanted me to do well in life."

"Yes, but there's more," my uncle replied. "Unfortunately, shortly after the ceremony you became a persistently sick child. Your life became a vicious cycle between death and life. One day you looked fine; the next you turned pale and yellow and looked as though you weren't going to make it. For two years, your parents did all they could to cure you. When nothing worked, they took you to your mother's father, who was a shaman.

"After performing a shamanistic ceremony, your grandpa had some good news. He determined you were sick because you were unhappy with your birth name. Name changes are common in Hmong society. Men sometimes change their names after they get married and have children to symbolize their transition to manhood. Other times, men change their names because they don't want bad spirits to recognize them. A name change might involve an elaborate ceremony, ritual, or celebration. Or a shaman might tie a red string around a person's wrist and give that person a new name and identity. Your grandpa renamed you Lee Pao. Afterward, your sickness went away, and you haven't needed a shaman since then. Is that correct?"

"Yes, that's right," I said. My name had been shortened from Lee Pao to Pao when I immigrated to America, although my close family members continued to call me by my birth name, Touger.

"See, it does work then, right?" he asked.

"Well, Uncle, to be honest, I don't really know. Maybe my grandpa's prescription worked. Or maybe I was going to get better anyway. Could that be a possibility as well?"

"I guess," my uncle said smiling. "I have more to say. Though you were a very spiritually needy and sick child, you were also a very lucky child. You were lucky because you were your mother's 'guardian angel.' She took you with her wherever she went, even to your poppy field. Your mom sometimes stayed there with you for days or weeks at a time.

"You became your mother's guardian angel in the early 1970s, when you were only a few months old. During the rainy season, it was common to see fog and clouds moving along the mountains and forests in the early morning. One day, your mom woke up early and took you out of the house. She boarded an old 1960s Russian truck that had been converted to carry passengers from village to village. The two of you were on your way to Long Chieng from our village near Phonsavan, though I don't know why. To keep you safe during the long ride, your mom wrapped you tightly to her bosom using a traditional Hmong baby carrier, which looks like a sling.

"As the driver drove along the winding mountain roads, something terrible happened, and the truck went over a cliff. It tumbled down a slope, tossing the passengers out. Many were crushed before the truck came to rest. Miraculously, you and your mother survived.

"When we got to the site, we discovered why you and your mother had lived. You had been the first ones tossed from the truck, and you landed in a deep hole that people had dug to remove tree and plant roots for medicine. The hole was several meters deep and several meters wide.

"After the accident, people began speculating that you and your mother had survived because you had been with her. So you became her guardian angel."

I couldn't hear more. I finished my beer and thanked my uncle.

"No problem," he replied. We went upstairs, I thanked him again, and I left.

I held back tears while listening to my uncle, and I held them back still when I left his duplex. They would have to wait until I got home.

A part of my past caught up with me that night. Hearing my uncle talk brought a clarity to some of my experiences that I had never had before. Once again, I felt that I had let my mother down when we were crossing the Mekong River, that I had failed her as her guardian angel when we were separated.

I couldn't sleep that night. I kept wondering why my mom and I had survived the crash only to go through much worse. Was it divine intervention? Or just luck?

Whatever the case, I hoped my good fortune would continue. I hoped all the running, starving, killing, and dying was behind me and that I wouldn't know more years of uncertainty and hopelessness in the future. Before falling sleep, I asked myself, "Life can't get any worse, can it?" Then I thought, "If it does, I'll need all the blessings from when I was born and all the fortune that has been with me thus far."

In the Hmong culture, our parents are our teachers, historians, philosophers, and supporters. With mine being gone, I couldn't wait to have more of these conversations with my uncle.

Epilogue

When there is love there is life.
—Ghandi

In the fall of 1986, I started my freshman year at Green Bay East High School. High school was a very busy time for me, when I finally found some consistency in my life through academics. I enrolled in a class that started at seven in the morning, before the start of the regular school day. Through rain, snow, and bone-chilling cold, I walked to school at six thirty every school day. My commitment to academics paid off when I graduated from high school in three years instead of four.

When I wasn't in school, I played basketball and soccer and ran track and field. I never had much luck with basketball and track and field, but I was an accomplished soccer player. I made the varsity team during my sophomore and junior years, earning a few honors as a midfielder for my play. When I wasn't in school or playing sports, I was working. I had many odd jobs. I worked as a custodian, picked cherries and apples, farmed cucumbers, washed dishes, and worked as an office assistant at a law firm.

After high school, though I still doubted whether a university was the right place for me, I started college at the University of Wisconsin–Green Bay in 1989. Because I had earned good grades in high school and came from a poor background, I received enough financial aid which made it possible for me to continue

At the Green Bay East High School graduation at Brown County Arena in June 1989, I was already contemplating what the future held.

my education. I suppose I did it as well because it felt like the next thing to do in life. Still, in many ways I continued to think of myself as intellectually and culturally inferior to my classmates. At the same time, based on what I had thus far achieved, I knew I was motivated and that, with enough perseverance, I could outwork my peers.

During my first two years at UW–Green Bay, the most important thing to happen to me was a moment when one day, while walking back to my dorm at midnight, memories that I hadn't recalled in years came back to me. I remembered my father's assassination, my mother's death, funerals, starvation, and feelings of hopelessness and sadness. That night the memories left me paralyzed, but over time they also ignited in me a commitment to understand my past in the context of the "paper world," in the languages and written records so different from the Hmong oral traditions in which I had been raised.

Not only did I start thinking about my past when I was in college, I started thinking more seriously about my future as well. In August 1991, I got married, not giving a second thought to any of the complications that come with marrying young. My wife's name is Maya, and yes, she's the same Maya I met in 1986 at a Hmong New Year celebration in Oshkosh, Wisconsin. Her father, like mine, had been assassinated, and that happened shortly after she was born. She comes from a large family, with three living older brothers and three living older sisters, all living across the United States. When we got married, she was twenty-four and I was nineteen, an age difference that is rare in Hmong culture. Traditionally, if a younger man married an older woman, it was usually because he was forced to marry the widow of an older sibling out of necessity in order to keep widows in the family. Yet I never gave Maya's age a second thought. As an orphan and a person who had learned to be independent from a young age, I had grown accustomed to doing things my own way, regardless of tradition.

Whereas Maya was doing well as a student when we met, I was contemplating dropping out of college. I had started to struggle academically and still didn't have the first clue why I was in college at all.

Thirty years later, I am surprised and humbled when I think about how far we've come since 1991, though I doubt Maya is as surprised as I am. She went on to earn a bachelor's degree in social work from the University of Wisconsin–Oshkosh and a master's degree in social work from the University of Wisconsin–Madison. I took a more circuitous route through my education.

Being named the varsity soccer head coach at West De Pere High School in 1990 helped set me on my path. The people who hired me must have seen something in the eighteen-year-old version of myself that I didn't. I coached varsity for two years, and in that time, I went from being shy and reserved to believing that I could lead and make a difference in the lives of others. The birth of our first child, Sterling, in 1992 also inspired me to keep going when I was thinking of giving up. Becoming a father jolted me out of the stupor I had been in and committed me to studying harder and learning more about what it takes to be successful.

I stuck with college, earning a bachelor's and a master's degree in education from UW–Oshkosh (where I transferred from UW–Green Bay) and a doctorate in educational administration from UW–Madison in 2001. Had I not coached soccer, I might never have majored in education, becoming the first in my family and clan to graduate from college. I might not have become a middle and high school teacher, administrator, and later a university professor. To this day, I am grateful to Dave Dobkoski, the athletics director at West De Pere who hired me.

My career has had its ups and downs, though, and I've experienced more failure than success. I was rarely interviewed for jobs, and when I was, I didn't do well. But I've always had support and encouragement from the organizations and people that have taken a chance on me, for which I'm very lucky. That said, I have my critics. Most educators do. I look past them, focusing instead on how proud I am that I get to shape students' futures in a positive way.

Many have done the same for me.

With success came new and unexpected opportunities. In 2004, I was selected to participate in the Fulbright-Hays study abroad program, a federal government program that funds the advancement of teaching and research abroad. I was chosen to work in

Southeast Asia. After more than twenty-five years away, I returned to Laos. I was so excited to be back in an ancient world far from America, where I was among all things Asian. Nevertheless, though I came back to the land where I was born, I felt like a stranger, an outsider who didn't belong. I couldn't speak Lao or Thai, and I dressed, looked, and moved like a foreigner.

I have since returned to Thailand and Laos several times. When I visited Phonsavan in 2018, I walked the streets that my grandparents and parents had once walked and looked upon the mountains and valleys they once looked at. I visited the Plain of Jars, a prehistoric site in Xiangkhouang Province of enormous cultural relevance. I thought about my parents, too. Had my father still been alive, he would have been in his eighties, while my mother would have been in her seventies.

My grandparents, Chiaseng Lor and Va Vang, Vang, Vue, and a cousin, in a photo most likely taken in Phonsavan, Laos. They would have walked an entire morning from their village to get to Phonsavan to have the photo taken. Decades later, I visited Laos to retrace some of their steps and connect to my past.

I was home yet far from it, a sentiment that many Hmong of my generation understand. I feel good that I can tell my children about their history in Southeast Asia, which they will one day share with their children. They are part of a history that goes back many centuries, to when our ancestors left China in search of a better life. They could not have known that one day their descendants would find what they were looking for much farther away, in "the heavenly kingdom above the clouds where cities glittered of gold."

Unlike me, my siblings have yet to go back to Southeast Asia, four decades after leaving Thailand. Unfortunately, Vang passed away in 2000, and Vue passed away in 2013, before they had a chance. Pheng, Kong, and I, along with our spouses, had planned to visit Thailand and Laos in June 2020. We had hoped to visit what's left of Ban Vinai and Ban Nong Khai, along with the places where we were born, where we grew up, and where our ancestors had ascended to heaven. Sadly, however, the COVID-19 outbreak disturbed our plans. It's unclear when my other siblings and I will see Asia again.

I am most proud of my siblings' achievements in the last four decades. Kong now lives in Green Bay with his wife and family, has two daughters and two sons, graduated with a master's degree in public administration, and works for the Social Security Administration. Pheng also lives in Green Bay with his wife and family, has three daughters and two sons, and has worked for Krueger International for almost two decades now. Yanghoua has two daughters and four sons, is retired from Georgia Pacific, has owned many businesses, and is currently in Oklahoma running a business. Vue, a devoted Christian, had four daughters and two sons and worked for the Green Bay Area School District for almost three decades. His wife, my sister-in-law, still lives in Green Bay. Vang and his wife raised a beautiful family of six daughters and five sons, and his children and their families are living in Wisconsin, Minnesota, California, and North Carolina. My sister-in-law has remarried.

My journey wouldn't have been possible without many people. To express my gratitude, I leave you with an ancient Hmong cultural practice of expressing gratitude and extending help to others, a tradition that still exists in Hmong communities today: Thank you for all your support. I'm sure there are many whom you could help, but when I called, you came. I am thankful and grateful. Should you or your family ever need my support, please don't hesitate to ask. I might not be able to help with money, food, or supplies, but I will be there to support you with all of my strength, courage, will, and whatever else my body and spirit can give.

Discussion Questions

1. Many Americans did not know about the Secret War in Laos as it was happening. How much did you know about the Hmong or the Secret War before reading this book? What would you like to learn more about now?
2. Pao Lor uses the jungle to represent both the difficult journey his family took in Laos and the challenges he experienced after arriving in the United States. What difficulties did he face as a young boy in the United States? How might these experiences have reminded him of an actual jungle?
3. Pao was very young at the time he left Laos for Thailand and then the United States. How did his age affect his experiences? How might this story have been different if told by an older relative, such as one of his teen brothers or adult uncles?
4. Oral storytelling is important in the Hmong culture. What are some of the different purposes these stories serve? How do you think stories that are shared out loud many times compare to ones that have been written down?
5. What role does storytelling play in your own family? Does your family have any stories about its history that have been passed down? How have these stories been shared from one generation to the next?
6. From all the stories Pao grew up hearing from his elders, why do you think he remembers the orphan tale the most and chose to retell it instead of other stories?

7. The author describes several incidents of racist bullying or name calling toward himself or others. How did such behavior affect students who experienced it? Have you witnessed or experienced anything similar? If so, how did it affect you?
8. Several teachers and coaches played a key role in Pao's early life. How did the actions of these adults affect him in positive or negative ways? Have any teachers or other adults outside your family had a big impact on you?
9. Why did Pao see himself as someone who was not meant for college, in spite of doing well at school? What factors held him back? What changed his mind?
10. Independence is a key theme in Pao's story. In what ways did his experiences force him to become independent from a young age? How did his independence help or hinder him as he grew older?
11. In the first chapter, Pao describes the life he was meant to lead if the war hadn't happened and he had grown up in Laos. How does that compare to the course his life ended up taking, and how does he seem to feel about that?
12. Late in the book, Pao seeks out his uncle for a conversation about his family history. Why was this important to him? How did finding out more about his past affect him?
13. Why did Pao decide to write this memoir? What value do you think his story has to other Hmong families in the United States? What do you think Americans who are not Hmong get out of reading this story or others like it?
14. What surprised you most about Pao's story? Were there any parts you could relate to?
15. If you could ask Pao one or two questions about his journey, what would you want to know?

Acknowledgments

I have to start out by thanking my ancestors, grandparents, parents, and siblings. Your hope, perseverance, and dream of a better life got me to where I am today. I am forever thankful.

I want to thank my two uncles for leading us from Laos to Thailand. The decision to leave your homeland knowing you may never return must have been difficult. I don't know if I could have made such a decision.

I especially want to thank Vang for taking care of me and my siblings after my parents died and making the decision for us to come to the United States. You sacrificed so much for us. I want to thank Vue for taking care of me when I was growing up in the United States. You always put my well-being ahead of yours and put me in the best circumstances to succeed, allowing me to play soccer, to participate in extracurricular activities at school, to be in a band, and to explore the world on my terms. I want to thank my sister Yanghoua for nurturing me during some of my most challenging times. When I was confused and lost, you were there to console me and renew my will and courage to keep going. I am most grateful. I want to thank my brother Pheng for his support and guidance as we grew up together. You loaned me your car, money, clothes, and anything you could give me so I could succeed. And I want to thank my brother Kong for his unwavering companionship, loyalty, and faithfulness. I needed so much of that, for my journey has often been a lonely one. I hope I have been a good role model for you.

Additionally, I want to thank my sisters-in-law (my brothers' wives) and my brother-in-law (my sister's husband) for your tireless support over the decades. You are caring, compassionate, and kind individuals.

I want to thank Maya, my wonderful, kind, and patient wife. You uplift and heal me, bringing so much inspiration, purpose, joy, and happiness to my life. I am the luckiest person on earth to have you as a wife. Thank you so very much!

I want to thank our children, Sterling, Phenix, Chynna, and Reeve. You are wonderful, kind, humble, and intelligent individuals. You contribute so much love and meaning to my life. I am proud to be your father, and I am very proud of each of you.

I want to thank my uncles, aunts, cousins, nephews, nieces, grandchildren, and in-laws (from the Lor clan as well as the other clans). Each of you has played a critical role in shaping me into the person I am today.

I want to thank our wedding negotiators, Norxwm and Tongpao of Green Bay; my best man, Txua of Green Bay; bridesmaid, Ntxawm of Merced, California; and everyone else on my wedding team for a successful and enjoyable wedding, the start of my life with Maya.

I want to thank my teachers. Special thanks to my first Hmong teacher in Nong Khai; Mr. Metz and Mr. Lass at Tank Elementary School; my dissertation chair, Dr. Clifton Conrad at University of Wisconsin–Madison; and my mentor and professor Dr. Scherie Lampe at the University of Wisconsin–Oshkosh. I never wanted to disappoint any of you. Thank you so much for believing in me, guiding me, and making me who I am.

I want to thank two of the greatest Hmong American leaders of my time: General Vang Pao and Dr. Yang Dao. I am grateful to have met and conversed with each of you and learned of your will, courage, sacrifices, and vision for the Hmong and their place in the world.

I want to thank my colleagues. Special thanks to Saroj Thekkanath and Dr. Muriel Hawkins for giving me my first professional opportunity, Don Schlomann for my first teaching job, Terry Fondow and Rob Bohm for my first administrative position, Mark Duerwaetcher for my administrative opportunity at Neenah High School, Dr. Steven Kimball at UW–Green Bay for being a friend, Dr. Ray Hutchison at UW–Green Bay for your collaborative partnership, and Dr. Tim Kaufman at UW–Green Bay for all your support during my tenure at UW–Green Bay.

I want to thank my soccer coaches. I especially want to thank Mr. Kenevan for giving me my first opportunity to play organized sports, my high school coach Bill Rincon, and my summer competitive coach Horst Stemke. You three believed in me, allowing me to play freely, never doubted my dedication, and put me in position to be successful. I want to thank my teammates and all the soccer players I practiced with or played pickup games with from the streets of Bangkok to the Mall in Washington, DC, and throughout northeastern Wisconsin.

I want to thank my former students and players. Each of you touched my life in many ways, and I hope I have done the same for each of you.

I want to thank everyone at the Wisconsin Historical Society Press. Special thanks to Kate Thompson for believing in the book, to my editors Tom Krause and Erika Wittekind for refining my voice and bringing so much clarity and substance to the story, and to everyone else at Wisconsin Historical Society Press for your support and guidance.

Finally, I want to thank everyone and anyone whom I might have missed or didn't mention by name. I am grateful that each of you has graced my life in one way or another.

About the Author

Pao Lor holds the Patricia Wood Baer Professorship in Education at the University of Wisconsin–Green Bay, where he also chairs the Professional Program in Education. He received his PhD in educational administration from the University of Wisconsin–Madison in 2001 and has been writing about the Hmong American experience for many years.

PHOTO BY DANIEL MOORE, UW–GREEN BAY